Natchez Mississippi Postscripts 1781–1798

Carol Wells

HERITAGE BOOKS
2011

HERITAGE BOOKS
AN IMPRINT OF HERITAGE BOOKS, INC.

Books, CDs, and more—Worldwide

For our listing of thousands of titles see our website
at
www.HeritageBooks.com

Published 2011 by
HERITAGE BOOKS, INC.
Publishing Division
100 Railroad Ave. #104
Westminster, Maryland 21157

International Standard Book Numbers
Paperbound: 978-1-55613-604-7
Clothbound: 978-0-7884-8890-0

FOREWORD

Within the sixty-eight pages of *Natchez Postscripts* are over five hundred fifty surnames, the given names of more than one hundred slaves, and fifty-five connections with other countries, states, counties, cities, and Indian nations.

Natchez Postscripts was abstracted from a typescript in the Cammie G. Henry Research Center of Watson Library, Northwestern State University of Louisiana. The typescript contains records purporting to have been translated from the Spanish and was typed from the handwritten eighteenth century translations. Some appear in May Wilson McBee, *The Natchez Court Records 1767-1805: Abstracts of Early Records.* Greenwood, 1953, repr. Balto, 1979. Most have not been published.

Problems abound in using *Natchez Postscripts.* I have not been able to locate the original records, and do not know if they still exist. Before I abstracted them, the documents had been copied by David Harper and had been typed by an unknown typist. Thus besides my own errors, two other chances exist for errors to have been made in reading names and dates. The typist wrote: "The Spanish regime in Natchez, Miss., dated from 1779 to 1798. These official documents were translated from French and Spanish into English by David Harper in 1818. So far as is known, these records from the longhand of David Harper were first put into typed form by this transcription made in 1944 in an effort to preserve what remained of the tattered originals and the 1818 translations."

Page numbers in *Natchez Postscripts* refer to the typescript in Watson Library. For unknown reasons the typist had rearranged the original pages so completely that their proper order cannot now be determined.

Names appear as spelled in the typescript. Brabaron & Brabazon are probably different readings of the same handwritten name, as are Thorn and Hiorn; Row and Rowe, Hankins and Hawkins. The reader should use this volume as an extended index to original records. The words "will of" mean "the last will and testament of" but this and many other phrases have been shortened. Likewise; all will abstracts omit the disposition of the body and the payment of debts.

The symbol + means the name appears on a page more than once. N.P. and N.D. mean no place and no date were in the typescript from which this book was made, possibly having been inadvertently omitted by the typist.

While most documents fall between the years 1781 and 1798, dates early as 1775 and late as 1816 are found.

p.1
Territory South of Ohio, Davidson County. Deposition of Wm. Tait made before John Gordon, a Justice/Peace for sd County. Tait knew Captain James Bosley in this County eleven years, and also knows him to have a mulatto slave named Carsey, who was stolen by an Indian Fellow, and taken down the river for a wife to sd Indian. Capt. James Hogget brought back sd mulatto girl, and further this Deponent saith not. Wm. Tait
Sworn before me - 29 June 1796 John Gordon, J.P.

Territory of United States South of River Ohio. Davidson Co. Andrew Ewing, Clerk of County Court, certifies that Jno Gordon is & was at the time of taking above deposition, a Justice of the Peace.... July 1st, 1796. Andrew Ewing

p.2
Petition of Anthony Hutchins. Last June he bought from Mr. Tomlinson a barrel of flour for himself and one for Mr.McIntosh. At the door of the house where McIntosh then lived, he desired Betsy who lived there to put his flour with Mr.McIntosh's. Later he was told his flour was stored at Mr.Bacon's by James Smith. Hutchins suspects collusion between Bacon & Smith, their testimony in trial against Bacon differing from that in the declaration taken by Mr.Fitzgerald & attested by Capt. McIntosh. Prays satisfaction what hath been done with the flour which Smith rolled somewhere else. [no date]

p.3
Natchez District. The Court of Requests, acting agreeable to the Capitulation of Baton Rouge holding the British Laws, To any lawful Constable. - Execution against goods and chattels of Jeremiah Hill to make Five Dollars Three Bitts to satisfy a Judgment which Silas Crane obtained against the sd Hill in the Court of Requests at November Term last. Witness Isaac Johnson, Esquire, one of the Justices of the sd Court.
Natchez, 5th December 1790. Will Fergursone, Clk.

Judgement	1.4
Clks. fees	2.2
Constables	1.4
Cryers	.1
	5.3

p.4-5
Undated declaration by Anthony Hutchins. Hutchins was notified by Constable Silas Crane to appear before Don Charles De Grand Pree to answer complaint of Wm McIntosh respecting

a note in favor of James Farlie of Pensacola. Hutchins on 5 Nov 1779 gave his note for his debt, note due from Alexander Boyd and another from Parker Carradine, expecting to receive the amounts from them. Same day he gave Farlie a draft for the amount on Messrs Bay and Macullagh, attorneys, who promised payment of sum. Hutchins supposes they paid the sum and he feels it unjust to pay it again. If it has not been paid, he desires time to recover the amounts from Boyd & Caradine. Hutchins is indebted to several persons and lost his property by misfortunes: first by Capt.Jas.Willing's party; second by the Sloop Catherine in the Mississippi, third by the late insurrection at the Natchez. He has struggled against banditts whose chief attorney is determined to ruin him.

p.6
Barbour & Harrison to Commandant Don Carlos de Grand Pre, 22 November 1781. Petition states that Caleb King of this District owes them seventy bushels of Indian corn, beg that the Commandant will order debt to be paid.

p.6-7
Petition of Anthony Hutchins, Oct.1781. After trial, Richard Bacon was ordered to deliver to Hutchins a saddle; instead he kept it hired out until today; now it is in an unfit condition which petitioner could not receive as pad was ruined, crupper was gone; Petitioner prays Bacon may be constrained to pay obedience to authority and justice may be done.

p.7
Received from James Jellison two sets of certificates on the government for 438 Dollars. Natchez, 1 Jan.1779, Alexander McIntosh

Alexander McIntosh to James Jellison. Interest from 15 March at which time Jellison paid John Miller above amount; 6 Dollars work done on wagon. Accounts, New Orleans, 15 May 1780

p.8
James Jelliason [mark] certifies 439 Dollars 6 Ryalls is due him, which he has not received. New Orleans, 15 May 1779.

Deposition of William Ferguson before John Blommart, Justice of the Peace for Natchez District. Alexander McIntosh, formerly Captain & Commanding Officer, Fort Panmure, from September 1778 until 10 December, received four bills/exchange from Board/Ordnance, Pensacola, on London, for work done at the fort from 1 September 1778 to 10 December, including the building of a block house and finishing another, work mostly done by James Jellison, amounted to 438 Dollars.

Will Ferguson certifies he had a warrant from Col.Commandant John M.Gillwray, to act as Clerk of the Garrison, date 24 or 25 Sept.1778 till 10th Dec, Alexander McIntosh commanding.

p.9
Natchez District. Deposition of Chas. Binghaman before John Blommart, Justice/Peace: last November Binghaman was at Mr. McIntosh's house when Jas. Jelliason demanded money McIntosh owed him for building block houses in Fort Panmure. Deponent heard McIntosh offer James Jellison a draft on John Miller, Esq. That not being satisfactory to the claimant, McIntosh promised to pay the cash in December following. Bingamon
Sworn before me, this 24th April 1780. Blommart.

p.9-10
Petition of Barbour & Harrison to Don Carlos de Grand Pre, 12 October 1778. Andrew Knotts, indebted to Barbour & Harrison, left property with Parker Caradine of Coles Creek which he says he purchased of Johnston;,such sale could only be to defraud his creditors as the property was disposed of at the time Knotts went off. Z.P.Harrison
Grand Pre orders attorney of Andrew K. Johnston or to Parker Caradine, who is to pay the accounts demanded.

p.10
Certification that a hogshead of tobacco sold & delivered by Jno Farquhar had net weight five hundred seventy nine pounds French weight, at rate of Eight Dollars per hundred weight, payable in merchandise. Charles Norwood
New Orleans, February 8th 1781.

p.10-11
Petition of Anthony Hutchins: a barrel of flour he purchased last June from Mr.Tomlinson, he ordered put in Mr.McIntosh's store. James Smith, employed by McIntosh, put it in Richard Bacon's house. Bacon denied flour was put in his house. Petitioner demands the barrel of flour; also Bacon unlawfully took petitioner's saddle and has detained it for 3 months.

p.11
Declaration of James Smith: A short time after Capt.Morande received possession of Fort Panmure, that he was at the door of that part of the house of Richard Bacon where Mr.McIntosh then lived, and saw two barrels of flour opened for Colonel Hutchins, one for use of Mr.McIntosh and the other for said Hutchins, and the one for Mrs. McIntosh was taken to her own store, the other was rolled part way toward same place, but being forbid taking it there for want of room, it was taken by sd Smith to Bacon's house, and rolled by Smith into same room where other flour was stored but on the opposite side,

the left hand, near and on the other side of the water tank. Smith had leave before he put the flour into the said house.
Natchez, 8th Oct. 1781 A. McIntosh G.W.Fitzgerald

Mr. William Case
To John Kennedy, Dr.
May 15 - 1781 To a large flour barrel taken by you
My property and not returned. $50.00

Natchez. Order for the fugitive Case's attorney to pay the charges demanded, or the Constable will seize Case's estate.
Grand Pre

p.12
Bill/Sale, John Rowe to Abraham Geney, both of Natchez Dist. 8 horses, 26 cattle, 21 hogs, plantation on St. Catherine's Creek, houses, fences, improvements. 400 Spanish mill dollars. 1779. Witness: Jas Peterkin, Caleb Hansbrough

Petition of Barbour and Harrison, 30 August 1781, says John Choate, late of this District, stands indebted. John Choate still has property in sd district. Petitioners being oldest creditors beg an order that debt may be paid. John Harrison

p.13
Natchez, 17 August 1781. Michael Hoopock's debt to Alexander McIntosh, it shall be paid at 8 percent interest. Grand Pre

Natchez, August 23, 1781. Patrick Foley and William Ferguson chosen to decide a dispute between Michael Hooppock and John Kennedy, asks Mr. Hooppock made good his receipt, Mr.Kennedy being Hooppock's clerk.

p.13-14
Don Charles De Grand Pre, Lt.Colonel, Commandant Civil and Military of the Post of Point Coupée and its District and by special Commission of the District of Natchez. Petition of Alex McIntosh, stating that he has a demand to make against Isaac Johnson, Esq. of this District, to the amount of Three Hundred Eighty Five Dollars and Four Bits. Petitioner waited a long time for his money. Begs sd Isaac Johnson be ordered to make immediate payment. Alexander McIntosh
Natchez, August 22nd, 1781.

Only satisfaction Petitioner has received for the within was a promise from Mr.Johnson to be in this day or tomorrow with a negro wench, which is not sufficient for the amount of the debt. Begs payment be ordered. Alexander McIntosh

Petition of Peter Hawkins to Charles De Grand Pre, Natchez, September 3, 1781. Hawkins lent Andrew Welsh a cow and calf. Welsh shot cow. Welsh is famous for killing neighbors cattle and making use of them, was condemned to gaol for 3 months, and it appears by Declaration of Richard Adams, he is going anew. Francis Farrell, interpreter.

p.15
Declaration of Richard Adams. I see Welsh come out of his house and load his gun. Then I see him creep away and shoot the cow. She came afterwards up to my house bleeding. They turned her out of the field, and my family. I see her still bleeding, and afterwards his wife came to my house and said she seen him put a bullet in the gun. Then she told him his eyes coveted to be killing something that was not his own.
Natchez, 3rd September 1781.

His
Richard (R.A.) Adams
mark

p.15-16
Natchez Dist., [blank] August 1781, before Don Charles Grand Pre, Anthony Hutchins declares that in 1778 Wm Vousdan purchased from John Row a plantation on Second Creek, which at that time was not secured by patent. Vousdan told him he had agreed with Jno Row at a certain price; Vousdan was to be at expense and trouble in procuring patent for sd land; Vousdan said Row was to sign him a deed, and to deliver receipt for money he had paid for fees to Wilton and others. Vousdan had given Row his bond for same, and he had paid a negro girl in part thereof; Vousdan requested deponant to apply to Surveyor General, who promised grant for said land. Hutchins left Pensacola without obtaining it.

p.16
Will Ferguson, acting for Vousdan, represents to Don Carlos De Grand Pre that in summer 1777 Vousdan sold Samuel Sweezy negro Romeo for 325 Dollars payable the summer following, & which Vousdan sent to Pensacola by John Miller who still has the bond. Vousdan has been long without his money and negro. He begs De Grand Pre to order the bond with interest be paid and negro returned. Natchez, August 30, 1781

p.17
Petition Wm Ferguson to Don Carlos De Grand Pre. October 2, 1781. Petitioner says Sweezy has sold the negro that was in dispute between him and Ferguson on behalf of Mr.Vousdan. He purposes to give the money to David Ross, attorney. Ferguson begs that Sweezy be made to follow Commandant's judgment.

p.17-18
Anthony Hutchins complains that he suspects that Mr.Hiser is

an unlawful person of evil practices, likely to be injurious to honest inhabitants of this district, their cattle, hogs, horses, being informed that Hiser lately killed a young unmarked bull, the property of someone of the neighborhood. He knows that it was not one of the stock that he said he purchased from Jacob Winfre. Hutchins, more than once, assured Hiser that there was but one unmarked creature belonging to Winfre's stock which he described to Hiser. Yet Hiser killed and converted to his own use the aforesaid bull, though said bull was never known to have run with said stock until a day or two before sd bull was slaughtered. Hiser enticed sundry hogs, property of Robert Robertson, deceased, and constantly fed and claimed them as his own, with intention to kill and convert them to his own use. And would have altered the mark of the hogs and put them into Winfre's mark, and desired his hireling to assist him, who refused to obey him in the unlawful act. Oct. 30 - 1781(?) Anthony Hutchins
Evidence to prove the charge are James Stanfield, [blank] Price, Richard King, and others.

p.18
Petition of Hannah Vousdan to Don Carlos De Grand Pre. Dispute over sale to Wm Coleman of sow with 5 pigs for 24 bushels of corn; sale to Emanuel Madison two sows for 41 bushels of corn. Madison, since death of Coleman, has management of Coleman's affairs. [illegible]

Anthony Hutchins opinion on suit of Richard Bacon. Whatever damage Bacon has sustained, Ellis is not culpable. No testimony appeared against him to prove his conduct unwarrantable in execution of his office as constable. August 28, 1781

p.19
Opinion of an Arbitrator in suit Richard Bacon agt Hardress Ellis: As attorney for Richard Bacon at the time of the sale of the corn in dispute, I protested against the sale as unlawful, and do now say so. But I cannot see how Hardress Ellis, having an execution signed by John Blommart, Esq, can be culpable for any loss sustained by Bacon. The estates of John Blommart & Donald McPherson are liable to make good the damage sustained by Bacon. July 1781. Isaac Johnson

William Pountney and George Rapalje are of opinion that said Bacon is entitled to damages as complained of against Ellis and are of opinion that said sale was illegal as appears by the Declaration of Isaac Johnson, Esq., one of the Justices of the Peace, then in Commission. Natchez, August 28th 1781.

p.19-20
Petition of Sam Henry: About seven weeks ago Petitioner sent

a silver watch from Coles Creek by hand of Earl Douglas to have repaired, and said Earl Douglas left the watch with one Billoo, a silversmith who resided at Jeremiah Brian's house. As said silversmith has deserted his country and carried off the watch which cost Thirty Dollars, which Petitioner got by his industry and as the sd Silversmith left property behind, Petitioner asks proper consideration. As proof that silversmith had sd watch, refer to Earl Douglas, Brian James Trisly, John Holt.

p.21
Petition of John Heathly to Don Carlos DeGrand Pre. Heathly has demand for 48 Dollars against Ruben Alexander, a planter of this District, whose negro stole this sum from him. Somehow Negro escaped to Baton Rouge where he was retaken. From a trunk that held Heathly and Alexander's clothes, Alexander took a packet of letters directed to Captain Foster. The Negro watched his opportunity and robbed Heathly of 100 Dollars cash, which was occasioned by his master's neglect. The negro has since been with Mr.Holloway. At Holloway's death the negro was sold. Alexander went to Baton Rouge to receive payment for sd negro. Alexander has no intention of settling with Heathly. Natchez. January 10, 1783

Francis Farwell, attorney for District of Natchez, says he found in the possession of sd negro fifty two dollars out of the hundred, also begs interest upon same for two years.

The subscribers say that when the accused negro was given up to English law, and escaped from officers of justice without his master's consent, said master is not liable to prosecution on his account. Natchez, Feb 7, 1782.
Isaac Johnson, Wm Pountney, [blank] Harrison

p.22
Agreement between George Furney, Natchez Dist., Province of West Florida, planter, and Bennet Truly, district & province afsd. Ten provisions of the partnership in building and operating a mill are outlined. Natchez, 24 November 1780.
Jacob Stampley, John Oran Bennet Truly.

p.23
S. S. Shell certifies he was present when Alexandre Graydon killed two of John Bisland's steers; & certifies that since Graydon came from Chickasauws Nation he told Shell to inform Mr. Bisland that he was willing to pay him for the cattle he killed or caused to be killed. Natchez, 24 April 1782

Petition of John Bisland to Don Charles De Grand Pre. States that Alexandre Graydon killed some beeves for use of himself and his company, which beeves were petitioner's property for which Mr.Graydon had no orders from his Commander, Mr. Blomart. Before Graydon set off for Chickasau Nation, he offered petitioner his note of hand before Mr. Spell for part of the beeves which he had killed. Before Mr.Bonner Graydon acknowledged he had killed four beeves belonging to petitioner for which Graydon owed eighty dollars. Graydon refuses to pay. Before Graydon returned from Chickasaw Nation, Groves Morris said that he had bought tallow from Mr.Graydon, from petitioner's beeves. Asks commandant grant equitable relief.

p.24
Opinion of Referees appointed to settle a dispute between Wm Weeks and Job Cory concerning articles of agreement signed 10 February last year: thirty dollars two ryals--the difference of accounts between Weeks and Cory--to be paid to Weeks by Cory; Weeks to deliver to Cory one half the increase of hogs in dispute. Cory to deliver all cattle to Weeks within two months. Natchez, 23 April 1782
Silas Crane, Wm McIntosh, Isaac Johnson
Natchez, 29 June 1782. Confirmation of above arbitration by Grand Pre.

Opinion of the Arbitrators between Mr.Shilling and Jno Short over a joint voyage New Orleans to the Natchez: Nine Dollars five Ryals are due to John Short. Unused provisions are to be equally divided. Patrick Foley, R.Bacon 12 December 1782

p.25
Natchez, 18 March 1782. Order by Grand Pre to George Forney and Mrs. Truly to render their accounts of expenses and receipts attending the will of Bennet Truly within three days.

p.25-26
Petition of Sarah Truly to Don Carlos De Grand Pre. Explains her position, as she is to pay George Furney out of Bennet's property. The first four years after her arrival, he was up the river hunting. William Ferguson paid Truly four calves. His only property was rifle he sold to buy a horse from Hopper. Sarah loaned him two horses, saddle cloth & money. All Bennet's cattle he killed, sold, or they died of distemper. She has no property of Bennet Truly's nor is any in the District. He bargained for the mill, but Sarah paid it. If she now has to pay Bennet's debts, she asks delay until crop is in, or she will have to sell a negro who will not bring its value, & her overseer will insist upon the number of workers the agreement calls for. Complaints against Forney.

p.26
Natchez District, 27 June 1781. Articles/Agreement between

Sarah Truly and George Tenney on the operation of her grist mill. Witness: Francis Spain

p.27
Petition of Sarah Truly to Don Carlos De Grand Pre. Agreement of Bennet and Furney concerns mill they began half mile above the Landing; when Capt.Harrison claimed the spot, they agreed to build a distance above, but without written agreement, as James Truly can prove. He can also prove that Bennet hired and paid 7 or 8 negroes to make a road from bluff to swamp for which Mr.Furney has given no credit.

Silas Crane to Elias Durnford, Surveyor General at Pensacola --pay William Williams or his order Crane's share of the fee for surveying four tracts of land for Captain Johnson, containing 5100 acres. Natchez. 7 June 1776

p.27-28
Will of James Perry, Natchez Dist., planter. To nephew Barnabas Perry, 3 cows & calves, bay horse, all real estate in Natchez Dist. Niece Rebecca Perry 3 cows & calves, sorrel mare. Nephew Daniel Perry 3 cows & calves, colt. Niece Ann Perry 3 cows and calves. Niece Lydia Perry 3 cows & calves. Residue to brother Daniel Perry, & Daniel executor. 19 March 1782. Wit: Isaac Johnson, Benjamin Holmes, Michael Hootor

p.28
Bill of Sale. Pat Lemons to Silas Crane for One Hundred Dollars, Black Mair four years old, year old mule coult, three year old mair of a bay culler, black stone horse, four years old. 6 June 1784 Pat Lemons In presence of John Marney

p.29
Natchez, 9 October 1783. Justus King and Sam W.Gibson certify that at John Lusk's on 4th inst. they saw the cow in dispute between Lusk and Silas Crane. Could not tell if brand C was upon L or L upon C. James Wilson said he and John Odom branded for Mr.Crane. At Lusk's plantation they put small c under WC on left cushion.

Natchez, 4 Oc^{t} 1783. John (x) Odom, Jonathan Andrews, Israel Leonard branded for Silas Crane at John Lusk's. Cattle formerly William Case's, sold at vendue. Subscribers viewed cow now in dispute between Crane and Lusk, believe branded for Crane. Also at same time they branded for Richard Devall, & remembrance not sure. Statement certified by Justus King

Natchez, 6 Oc^{t} 1783. Justus King and Sam W. Gibson consider most evidence is in Crane's favor.

p.30
Natchez, 7 August 1783. In above dispute, John Heathley believes C was placed upon L.

Natchez, 17 July 1783. William DeWit and William Rollings declare that two Calvits, sons-in-law of Higdon, did bet on Cobb's horse, to which horse Higdon, a judge, gave the race.

Natchez, 17 July 1783. Joseph Newton & James Finley declare that Richard Breshares, son-in-law of William Brocurs, bet on Cobb's horse, to which Brocurs, a judge, gave the race.

p.30-31
Petition of John Farguson. He bought eight thousand staves from John Short to be delivered by Peter Hankins on first of May last. Farguson sent a cooper to receive staves who found them unsatisfactory. Began suit before Grand Pre, who sent John Rowe to inspect the staves. Hawkins then delivered Jno Row a quantity of Richard Bacon's staves. He obtained judgment agt petitioner for the staves. Petitioner already paid Short for sd staves but never received them, though Bacon's staves had been their property, 1605 staves.

p.31
Request of John Harmon; he rented part of field which he had hired last year of Mr.Fugerson to Abram Scruggs and J.Thomas Andrews. They agreed to pay Mr.Fugerson proportional rent, & Harmon asks they be made to pay [no date]

Petition to Grand Pre. 6 Fe[b] last the petitioners hired with Paulser Shilling to row to New Orleans and back to Natchez for four bitts per day from 6 Fe[b] to March 31 when they returned; beg that Shilling be made to pay [no names, no date]

Undated and unsigned political commentary

p.32
Promissory note, Joseph Small to James Morrison, 60 pounds Virginia currency Dollars at six shillings each, guineas at 28 shillings each and in proportion for other gold or silver coin against 1st October next with legal interest till paid. 1 May 1788. Wit: Joseph Barnett, James Adams. Endorsed on back: New Orleans, 21 March 1790. James Morrison assigns all right to within note to Anthony Grass

p.33
Declaration. A yearling calf which Mr.Bacon claims, now in possession of Mr.Baker, is the very calf that Baker's family drove up in company with Baker's cattle, past Mr. Youltney's

plantation, sometime in March last, where I then lived.
Natches, Miss. June 30th 1783 Sarah D. Kelly (mark)

Petition of William Ferguson to Lieut.Governor Pedro Quinas: Ferguson and Stephen Mays agreed to make a crop together on Mayes plantation this season, but Mayes has not signed Articles of Agreement; requests Mayes be ordered to appear and comply with his agreement with Petitioner.
May 12th 1783 Will Ferguson

Petition of William Ferguson to Don Carlos De Grand Pre. Jno Turner owes estate of Wm Vousdan 70 dollars for cattle sold to him 2 March 1780. As Turner has property in this District Ferguson wants debt paid with interest. Natchez, 2 Jan[y] 1781

p.33-34
Will of Robert Robertson, Natchez Dist., West Florida. Moveables to be sold. Land to his eight children: Robert, Rhoda, Phebe, Mary, Briant, Caleb, Joseph, John or survivors if any do not live to age 21. Also equal parts of debts. Friends Justus King and Richard Swazey Jr executors. 10 Oct[r] 1777.
Witnesses: Silas Crane, Caleb King, Gabriel Swayze

p.34
William McIntosh of Natchez District, having some thought of going from hence to New Orleans to settle some accounts, and being in tolerable good state of health, sound judgment and memory, make my Last Will and Testament, in the name of God. Wife Unis McIntosh, sons William McIntosh, James McIntosh, & daughter Mary McIntosh, all my worldly substance and effects of any nature. Executrix to carry on plantation and business for four years; then to be valued and each to receive their part as is hereafter set down: Wife Unis McIntosh one third during her life; then to her two sons William and James and daughter Mary or their survivors, share and share alike. The other two-thirds to William, James and Mary, share and share alike. [--] January 1783. Wm. McIntosh
Witness: Alexander More, Joseph Homes, Benjamin Homes

p.35
Will of Sterling Spell, Natchez Dist., West Fla, planter. To wife Susannah all estate during widowhood, then to children Martha Spell and Benjamin Spell or their survivors. Should widow remarry, estate to be deposited with of George Rapalje and Samuel Gibson for benefit of children and they to act as guardians and executors of will. 12 November 1784.
Witnesses: John Shunk, Richard Ellis

Natchez, 5 Sep[t] 1788. Certification by James Elliott that three years ago he had beem charged by Mr. Trevino to settle estate belonging to orphans of Mr.Fulsom, deceased, at Coles Creek. Mr. Cato West on behalf of Mrs. Murdock and Elliott settled the accounts between Mrs.Murdock and the estate, and at sundry times Elliott asked Edmund Fulsom, eldest orphan, to recollect all property belonging to the estate that had been consumed while in the possession of Mrs. Murdock or her husband who was Fulsom's executor but was then dead. Edmund Fulsom answered that everything he recollected was mentioned in the settlement. Within 2 or 3 days, I sent Edmund and a negro to assist him with two horses and a slide to bring the property belonging to the estate from Murdock's to my house. He delivered some, and did not mention anything left at Murdock's. In a short time, at request of orphans their affairs were given to Jeremiah Bryan.

p.35-36
6 March 1789. Cato West certifies that when he took the inventory of the estate of Israel Fulsom, deceased, as ordered by Mr.Trevino, then Commandant, not all cattle were present.

p..36
Power/Att^{y} Thomas Green, Natchez Dist., to sons Thos Moreton Green, Cato West, Abner Green. 6 June 1784. Wit: Jno Eldergill, Joseph Stanley, John Smith. Philipe Trevino

10 September 1784 Agreement between Osborn Spriggs and James (x) Cole Junr both of Natchez, Province of Louisiana: terms under which Cole to care for Spriggs's horses for two years. Wit: Stephen Minor, Antonio Totents(?)

p.37
17 August 1781 Petition of William (x) Brochus shewing that Benjamin Day, late of Natchez but now absconded, received of Brochus last March eleven good hides to tan same and return half to Brochus but failed to do so.

Natchez, 26 August 1781. Silas Crane advertises for sale at publick vendue Benjamin Day's horse, to satisfy Wm Brochus in consequence of a judgment obtained by Brochus

25 July 1781 Deposition of Anthony Brabaron In August 1779, speaking to Wm Clark concerning a small yellow cow, Brabaron asked Clark whose cow she was. Clark replied, "she was once mine but I made a present of her to Mr. Jordan."
Taken before Isaac Johnson

p.37-38
Deposition of Sarah Holmes, 26 July 1781. At the time James Willing came down the river, her son Joseph asked her to get Twenty Dollars from Wm Clark. Clark had no money, but Joseph

owed money to Stephen Jordan, & if Clark took Joseph's note in Jordan's hand for Twenty Dollars, that would serve. Jordan sent the note. Sarah knows nothing of a sale between Wm Clark or Stephen Jordan. Taken before Isaac Johnson

B/S Seth Winslow to Richard Bacon, all Indian corn now on plantation of widow Anna Thompson. 2 February 1775

Deposition Anthony Brabazon before Don Chas De Grand Pre. On the day the corn was sold he went with Mr.Blommart and heard Mr.Wells forbid the sale of the corn. Mrs.McIntosh insisted upon the sale, would indemnify Ellis. Witnesses Francois Farrell, William Hubbard

p.38-39
Natchez District. Personally appeared before me Don Charles De Grand Pre, Lt.Col., Commandant Civil & Military of Point Coupée and District, and by particular Commission of Natchez District,-- Patrick Foley with a Declaration of the quantity of Corn delivered to the Constable, one hundred & [--] nine bushels and a half agreeable to the Constable's Declaration. July 23rd 1783. Witnesses Francis Farrell, William Hubbard

p.39
Natchez District. Personally appeared before me, Don Charles De Grand Pre, Lieut &c, William Hubbard, being present when Richard Bacon bought and paid the whole amount of sd corn to sd Winslow before Court made out judgment obtained by Alex^r McIntosh against Winslow. He also heard him say that as soon as he carried his raft down and sold it, he would return and pay the said McIntosh. Wit: Francis Farrell, Wm Hubbard

Natchez District. Personally appeared before me, John Blommart, one of the Justices to keep the peace for sd District, Samuel Wells, who swears that some time after Col.McGillray, leaving Natchez landing in June 1778 bound for Manshack with his men, certain corn of Richard Bacon's that Bacon bought & paid for from Seth Winslow, Bill of Sale bearing date Feb.2d 1778, was sold at public vendue, being first advertised that deponent, Bacon's Attorney, forbade said sale, & was obliged to bring sd Bill of Sale and his Power for so acting. Notwithstanding, another advertisement was put up the same day; the corn was sold at 2½ bitts per bushel, bid off by Mrs.Ann McIntosh; Constable Hardy Ellis would not have sold sd corn had not Ann McIntosh told him she would stand between him & all damages. Had not the sale been made this deponent could have got and had sold sd corn to the King for five bitts per bushel. 7th December 1780 Samuel Wells

p.39-40
Deposition of Isaac Johnson. Early 1778 Richard Bacon told Isaac he was going to New Orleans for few months on business & I agreed to act as his attorney. He had bought corn from Seth Winslow at widow Ann Thompson's. Meantime Alexander McIntosh obtained judgment ag[t] Winslow at Feb[y] C[t] 1778. Mrs. McIntosh insisted on taking possession of the corn. Johnson protested the sale. 27 April 1780

p.40
Deposition of Hardress Ellis, constable. An Execution behalf Alexander McIntosh was levied on corn said to belong to Seth Winslow. Samuel forbid sale. Ann McIntosh said her husband Alexander left her to act in his business, and she would pay all damages that should befall the sale, so it sold at 28 ½ ryals per bushel. 27 April 1780. J.Blomart J.P.

p.41
Petition of John Row. Wm Vousdan bargained for Row's place, Mrs.Jn[o] Lum being present. The Agreed price was Five Hundred Eighty Five Spanish milled dollars. Row has received Three Hundred sixty, and says Vousdan intends to defraud him.

William Vousdan of Natchez District, West Florida, Land Surveyor, bound to Jn[o] Row sum One Thousand Two Hundred Spanish milled Dollars to be paid to John Row 3 Feb 1778. Condition if Wm Vousdan pays John Row Five Hundred eighty five Spanish milled dollars 25 January next for 250 acres where John Row now lives on Second Cr, John Row is to make Wm Vousdan title in Fee Simple. Witnesses Jn[o] Lum, Jacob Winfree, Jacob Cobun

p.42
West Florida. John Row of Natchez Dist., planter, bound unto William Vousdan, sum One Thousand Two Hundred Spanish milled dollars. 3 Feby 1778. Condition, upon payment of 585 Dollars Row will make over to William Vousdan the 250 acres whereon Row lives. Wit: John Lum, Jacob Winfree, Jacob Cobun

Grand Pre: Mr.Farquher forbidden to move his property out of this District until he makes final settlement and defence.

p.43 Alex[r] McIntosh requests Monsieur DeGranpre to stop the proceedings Bacon ag[t] Ellis until McIntosh can appear in his own behalf. Natchez, 24 July 1781

February 1778, Mr. Bacon bought about 200 bushels corn from S.Winslow which he paid for. Mr.Bacon went to New Orleans & in April returned to Natchez where he stayed about a week.He ordered Mr.Wells his Attorney to send the above corn to the Fort, the price then being 5.25 pr bushel. Bacon set off to

New Orleans on 3 May, leaving Wells to deliver the corn. The corn was levied upon and sold at public vendu on pretence of an Execution against Seth Winslow, when in reality no Execution could be legally taken out at that time as a total stop was put to proceedings at the English Court from Feb[y] 1778 when Captain Willing came down till Jan[y] 1780. Jean Short

[no name or date] Hardy J. Ellis, constable who levied upon & sold the corn, says he did so by Court order, which proves false by his deposition taken by Mr.Blommart; he was forbid selling by Blommart, Johnson & Wells. I verily believe the execution would not have been taken out had the clerk of the Court been sober when he gave it as is pretty evident by the manner in which the execution is written. Mr.McIntosh seems to think I bought the corn to wrong him; my only desire was to purchase the corn for food.

p.43-44
Joseph Homes, Natchez District, remembers leveling execution on property of Seth Winslow then inhabitant of this district which I requested Hardis Ellis to see measured, corn sold by execution upon declaration of Wm Hubbard who showed the crib where the corn was lodged, being then Winslow's property, about mid June 1778. Witness: Jacob Winfree, Wm McIntosh

p.45
Petition, William Ferguson To Don Carlos De Grand Pre, Your petitioner being a principal creditor of William Vousdan and he being sent away, M. Delavillebeauve put the Management of his affairs in my direction. As that estate is indebted to petitioner, he asks that Grand Pre will invest him with the same authority. The woman cannot settle the affairs as they ought to be. She applies to petitioner for assistance in any estate affairs, but before petitioner interferes, he desires authority. Natches, July 30th 1784. Will Ferguson

Petition of Mary Carradine to Don Carlos De Grand Pre. Mary was widow with 3 children when she married Parker Carradine. She had 4 negroes and much property belonging to her 3 children. Now she has 8 children, expects 9th, is destitute of property and without subsistence. March 5, 1781

We order Gibson Clark, chosen by William Smith; Thos. Green, chosen by me; & Wm Rosswell Magget, chosen by Geo. Rapalje, to appraise the crop standing on the plantation GeorgeRapalje bought of Wm. Smith, what by order of Government will be delivered up to Richard Bacon, Natchez, June 1782. Trevino.
In obedience to above order we appraised crop as it stands to forty dollars. James Harmon, Thos. Green, Roswell Wyatt

p.46 Statement of account, Adam Bingaman to William Vousdan: To am[t] of Negro man Tom Terry sold by Alex[r] McIntosh without authority; To cash you paid Patrick Clemans; to interest.

Report of Arbitrators appointed by Comd[t] Philipp Trevino to settle Adams Bingaman against W[m] Vousdan: af[sd] Adams Bingham owes Vousdan 172 dollars 60 rials. 3 March 1784

p.47

Certificate of Sam W.Gibson, chosen by William Dartt and Jno Burnett as one of the judges to determine the distance on a race run by William Dartt and Burnett. I declare Burnett's horse gained the race. In said race was some dispute of Burnett's horse not keeping the road. I myself returned to the paths to measure a second time the distance between horses. After allowing for Burnett's horse turning out of the road, I again declare that Burnett's horse was considerably before the other. 23rd day of Jany 1785. Sam W. Gibson

Letter from Evans and James Jones, New Orleans, La., 16 Aug. 1784, to George Castles. Castles letter of 6th past, acknowledging receipt of Jones' letter of 20 May covering Moore's receipt for a bale of blankets. Notes of Thomas Reed and Jno Bisland are overdue. Macarty's vessel brought no blankets; considers prices. Evans and James Jones

Letter from George Castles to Dear Sir. Natchez, August 15th 1784. Has received bale of blankets from Mr. Moore, but has not opened them for fear moths should get into them. Mr.Reed says if you will send his note he will pay immdiately. After a spell of dry weather, crops have a bad appearance. Recent rain gives hope that tobacco crop will be one-half more than we expected three weeks ago. George Castles

pp.48-50

Rules from Don Manuel Gayoso De Lemos, Colonel & Commandant Civil & Military of the Natchez and its Dependencies, about fencing animals and erection of animal pens or pounds. Persons hereafter mentioned have power to call together the inhabitants to erect said pens, taking timber for the purpose where it can most conveniently be had with the least disadvantage to those from whom it must be taken. One pen each to be erected by I.Gaillard & A.Ellis; Samuel Hutchins & J. H. White; D.Williams and J.Lintot; R.Bacon & Tomlinson; R.Sweazy & P.Shilling; D.Grafton & I.Bernard; C.Boardman, W.Pipes; -- Bonner & T.Jorden; A.Bealle & J.Girault; I.Lum & N.Ivy; A. & I. Henderson; J.Calvet & Belk; Coleman & I.Foster; R. King and B.Curtis; I.Johnson & R.Ford; S.Heady & Ogilsby; I. Armstreet & T.Morgan; J.Minor & S.Holms; -- Scantling & C. King; P.Prestley & I.Cartin

p.50
Elizabeth (X) Stillee certifies she heard Wm Duett, sometime in 1783, say that he had not yet given anything to his wife or children. Elizabeth also heard James White say before his death that Mr. Duett asked him to witness a deed/gift he had made to wife & children of all his property. White would not sign & told Duett that it was wrong; he was trying to cheat his creditors out of their just debts. 4 February 1785. Witness: John Blommart

p.51
Elizabeth Raby certifies that she heard Mr.William Duett say he had never given anything to his wife or children. 4 Feby 1785. Witness: John Burnett

John Lovelace deposes that last September Wm Dewitt sent for him to make Deed/Gift of all his negroes to his wife & children, giving the name of Justice/Peace John Sumter, desiring to antedate sd writing 1st January 1781, which Lovelace did. Natchez, 6 March 1785. Witnesses: William Smith, James Armstrong, Estevan Minor

North Carolina, Burk County. Deed of Gift, William DeWitt to Catherine White: Negroes Ben, Filis, Jinny, and Mary; to my daughter Catherine DeWitt Negroes Febe and Sambo June. To my son Jesse Negroes Cuffey, Stephen, Eudgo, Manday, James, Dol and Lammenton; to my daughter Martha Negroes Filis and her child, and Jupiter. 1 January 1781. Witness: John White, Benjamin White, Joseph White, Thomas White

p.52
John Still Lee certifies that Wm DeWitt asked John White and wife to go to New Orleans to testify that deed/gift to wife & children was just. White asked Comdt for a passport, but was required first to pay his debts. White asked John Still Lee to be security for money owed Alex.Moore; he would repay because Wm DeWitt would pay White upwards of 100 Dollars for his trouble. Natchez, 5 February 1785

November 25 [no year]. J. Fitzpatrick to Sir[no name]. Order you gave Wm Smith on George Rapalji the 8th last January, it being balance due on Joseph Dawes note, was never accepted. Has sent order to Adam Bingaman with request it be paid.

I promise to pay Peter Hawkins 65 Dollars on demand. George Rapalji. January 8, 1785

In January next, I promise to pay Peter Hawkins 150 Dollars. 8 January 1785. George Rapalji

p.53
Deed. Peter Hawkins, of Natchez District, to George Rapalji, purchaser for Janet Rapalji, 200 acres five miles from mouth of Coles Creek granted to Jacob Paul, and 200 acres granted to Ebenezer Gaspit, for sum Three Hundred Dollars. 8 January 1785. Witnesses Parker Carradine, William Gilbert

Ja.Robertson, New Orleans, 4 Jany 1781, to Sir[no name] Robertson not returning by way of Natchez, requests business be settled with Mrs.Sarah Truly who has two of Robertson's cows with increase which she refuses to give up. Comdt granted a summons, but Robertson could not get her to trial before he left; she cannot deny receiving cows from Robertsons brother knowing them to be Robertsons. She has no bill/sale for them should she claim to have bought them.
Before I. Montgomery Jas. Robertson makes oath he never sold said cows to any person whatever.

Lieut.Robertson to Sir[no name]. Will Smith's wife can witness that she was present when the cows were delivered to me by her husband.

p.53-54
[no name] empowers Benjamin Balk to act with regard to Power of Attorney.
In virtue of within Power/Attorney and declaration of James Robertson, orders to Mrs.Sarah Truly to deliver sd cows and increase to Benjamin Balk. Fort of Natchez, 10 November 1781 Grand Pre

p.54
[no date] Jn° Montgomery to Oliver Pollock, Agent for the U. S. of America at New Orleans. Pay Benjamin Belk 39 Dollars, board for one officer & soldier; charge to State of Virginia

[no date. no signature] Declaration that the writer brought Betty & Jude in late 1772 or early 1773 from Carolina to the Natchez, bought of Richard Farr, indentured to age 21, born free of a free mulatto woman. They were taken from writer by Capt Willing's plundering party, took their indentures also.

20 Octr 1785. Richard Harrison certifies he was at the White Cliffs on 20 February 1778 when Isaac Johnson sold to James Willing a bay horse for 150 Dollars, William Thorn, security

p.55
12 April 1780. Sterling (X) Spell, Natchez District, deposes before John Blommart, Justice/ Peace for Brittanic Majesty, that 24 February 1778 he was present at White Cliffs Landing

when James Willing bought a horse from Isaac Johnson, Esq., for 150 Dollars. Johnson and Willing went to Wm Thorn, Esq. Willing asked Thorn to pay Johnson, and Thorn said he would.

New Orleans, 31 Jany 1782. William Vousdan certifies that Wm Hiorn, Es^{q} told him in Capt John Blommart's house at Natchez that he was security to Isaac Johnson, Es^{q}, for a horse that James Willing bought. Hiorn(Thorn?) promised to pay for it.

12 April 1780. Deposition of Ephraim Thornell, Natchez Dis^{t}, before John Blommart, Es^{q}, one of Brittanick Majesty's justices. On 24 Feby 1778 at White Cliffs Landing, Thornell was present when James Willing bought a horse from Isaac Johnson for 150 Dollars, Wm Hiorn Es^{q}, security for payment who said "I will pay Mr Johnson One Hundred and Fifty Dollars for the Horse on your account."

p.56
New Orleans, 31 Jany 1785. Isaac Johnson petitions Go^{v} Miro for redress: 24 Feby 1778 at White Cliffs as James Willing was preparing to leave for New Orleans, he sold him a horse for 150 Dollars. William Hiorn said, "I will pay one Hundred and Fifty Dollars to Mr Johnson on your account." Petitioner asked Hiorn(Thorn?) for the money at different times, before he left this country, received evasive answers, no money.

p.56-57
1 March 1785. Deed/Gift, Mary (M) Higdon, Natchez District, to her son Jeptha (x) Higdon, all property & slaves Old Tom, Young Tom, Dick, and Limbrick, reserving for her use during her life some slaves & animals. Should son die, one Negro to his widow, others revert to Mary Higdon. Witness: Stephen Minor, D. Smith

p.57
4 November 1784. Jesse Carter, Thomas Carter's son, sold his share of merchantable tobacco to John Bisland for 9 Dollars per hundred, French weight, and 20 Dollars for John Bisland to finish the crop, Jesse Carter being ailing.

p.57-58
21 Jany 1784. Agreement between John Bisland, Natchez Dist., West Fla., & Jesse Carter: Jesse contracts to work for Bisland in making a crop. Wit: John Farquhar, George Fitzgerald

p.58
Natchez, 29 January 1785. Inventory estate of Jesse Carter: bushels of corn, sweet & Irish potatoes, tobacco ropes, horses. John Bisland

p.58-59
23 March 1785. John Burnett of Natchez District, to St.Germain, for 800 Spanish Dollars payable 1 January next, 2/3 of a saw mill on or near land of Richard Goodwin, and same part of everything belonging to the mill. Witness: M. Marmadue

p.59
31 Jan[y] 1785. Will of Isaac Lewis. Estate to my brother Abel Lewis, all now in hands of Stephen Stephenson and there to remain by contract until next January. Horses at the Oppalusaw. Executor James Cole. Wit: Wm Ball, Abraham (x) Roberts, Stephen (x) Stephenson

p.60
Charles Trudeau, Surveyor General, Province of Louisiana. By decree of Stephen Miro, Governor General, lays out in favor Mr.J.H., 1000 arpents in Natchez District, on Second Creek, bounded by [blank], conforming to certificate of Deputy Surveyor Wm Vousdan of 11 March last. 28 February 1788

29 February 1788, New Orleans. Certification by Stephen Miro of foregoing survey granted to Mr.T.H. on Second C[k], bounded by Mr.A.H.I.Winfred and Daniel Clark. By order, Andrew Lopez

p.60-70
Essay on the Right of Suffrage

p.71
As umpire in a matter of controversy between Alexander Moore and Doctor McCabe, I have attended as well to the different opinions of John Girault and George Fitzgerald, the original arbitrators, and circumstances on either side [obliterated]

Petition. Wm Chambers, Att[y] for Joseph Thornton of N[o] America, to Gov.Gayoso. Dr.James Beatty, formerly of Kentucky, on 28 March 1790, purchased from Jos.Thornton flour, bar iron, steel castings and farming utensils, on credit of $258.11.5 Pennsylvania Currency, exclusive of interest, & equal to 689 dollars and 2½ Ryals, part of which property: a stud horse & hardware, was put into hands of Ezekiel Forman, of Natchez District, attorney for af[sd] Doctor James Beatty.

Petitioner, empowered by Joseph Thornton, begs order may be granted him to settle with & take possession of property left with Ezekiel Forman. Also an order to take possession of 31 dollars 4 rials due from Lawrance Miskler to Dr. James Beatty, note dated 24 May 1790, now in hands of David Ferguson, provided property afsd does not exceed balance due Joseph Thornton. Natchez, 26 July 1792 William Chambers

Mr.William Chambers will present the Power of Attorney & the account mentioned in the Petition; if it is not certified by the Spanish Minister or Consul in the United States, will at same time bring responsible persons of this District who are acquainted with the signatures to prove them. Gayoso

The Demand of Joseph Thornton appearing to be just by Documents presented by Mr.William Chambers, who is authorized to make demands, settlements, & give receipts for Joseph Thornton for property that Dr. James Beatty left to the charge of Ezekiel Forman, Esq., he will declare what property is actually in his possession, and will settle with s^{d} Chambers for same; settlement shall be recorded in the government office, for the safety of all parties. Gayoso

p.72
Bayou Sara District. Reuben Denham's deposition states that he was in fear of bodily hurt from Abraham Horton, also that Horton would burn his dwelling house or an out-house; prays protection of law. Order that for Denham's safety, Abraham Horton is to give security 1000 Dollars or be committed to Prison. 14 June 1797. H.Hunter, Daniel Clark, Alcaldes

Declaration by Ruben Dunham before Danl Clark, Alcalde. Dunham had a dog lately killed, believes by Abraham Horton, his son Nathan, or someone they employed. Neighbors knew dog to be a valuable animal and security to hogs and calves against bear, tygers and wolves; deponent is in bodily fear of Abraham and Nathan Horton; prays protection of law against them. Clarksville, June 12th 1797. Reuben Denham

To Elisha Hunter, Constable. Bring Abraham Horton and Nathan Horton to be dealt with according to law, on Wednesday, 14th inst., warrant this 12th June 1797. Daniel Clark, Alcalde

Province of Louisiana, District of Bayou Sara. Reuben Denham swears he is afraid Abraham Horton will burn or cause to be burnt the deponent's dwelling house or his out buildings and prays for the protection of the law. R. D. Denham
Sworn to before me, 13th June 1797. H. Gunter, Alcalde

p.73
Promissory note John Marney to Phillip Turpin. Natchez, July 12, 1788. Marney is to pay Phillip Turpin, Decr 10 next, 207 Dollars three bitts in merchantable tobacco, market price,to be delivered at the landing; on failure thereof, to bear 8% interest untill paid. Attest: William Barland, John Short

[Illegible] A report has been propagated by sundry persons against Reuben Denham, of Bayou Sara, and his daughter Elizabeth, highly injurious to their characters....

Buffalo District, 14 June 1797. Reuben Denham of Bayou Sara Dis^{t}, planter, prays Alcaldes H^{y} Hunter & Danl Clark permission to prosecute Benjamin Kimball, Merchant, for calumniating his character, prays protection and reparation.
In presence of Daniel Ogden, Zekariah Smith

Reubin Denham is to present charges against Benjamin Kimball at next meeting, Saturday the 17th instant at Clarksville.
H. G. Hunter, Daniel Clark, Alcaldes

Government of Natchez, District of Buffaloe. June 17th 1797. Reuben Denham, Bayou Sarah, before Alcaldes Henry Hunter and Danl Clark, declares Benjn Kimball has injured his character by insinuations that he debauched his daughter and aided her destroy child of which she was encient; asks reparation.
In presence of Daniel Ogden, Zachariah Smith

p.74
Reubin Denham vs Benjamin Kimball. Slander. Undersigned Alcaldes, diffident of legal knowledge, doubtful of authority in cases of such magnitude, refer the parties, with Denham's application, to His Excellency Don Manuel Gayoso de Lemos.
Daniel Clark, H. Hunter, Alcaldes

Government of Natchez, District of Buffalo. 14th June 1797. Reubin Denham, Bayou Sarah, planter, g^{dn} of daughter Elizabeth, before H^{y} Hunter and Danl Clark, Alcaldes, prays prosecution of Benjn Kimball of District af^{sd}, merchant, for defamation of Elizabeth's good name, and prays reparation.
In presence of Daniel Ogden, Zechariah Smith, Witnesses

Reubin Denham is present charges against Benjamin Kimball at our meeting Saturday 17th ins^{t} at Clarksville. Daniel Clark, H. Hunter, Alcaldes

Government of Natchez, District of Buffaloe. June 17th 1797. Pursuant to our order of the 14th instant, Reubin Denham on behalf of his child Elizabeth Denham, before Alcaldes Daniel Clark & Henry Hunter, declares his daughter's character has been irreparably injured through the malice of Benjamin Kimball, disseminator of falsehoods, prays Kimball make amends.
Reubin Denham In presence of Daniel Ogden, Zecharia Smith

p.75
Gov^{t} of Natchez, Dis^{t} of Buffaloe, 14th June 1797. Reubin Denham, Bayou Sarah, planter, g^{dn} of dau. Elizabeth, before Alcaldes H^{y} Hunter & Danl Clark, asks to prosecute Abr^{m} Horton, planter, for having defamed Elizabeth's good name.
In presence of Daniel Ogden, Zachariah Smith

Denham's application admitted; he is to present charges ag^{t} Horton at our next meeting which will be Saturday 17th inst. at Clarksville. Daniel Clark, H. Hunter, Alcaldes

Gov^{t} of Natchez, Dis^{t} of Buffaloe. June 17th 1797. Reubin Denham in behalf of dau Elizabeth age sixteen, declares that Abraham Horton at various times & in various companies traduced Elizabeth's character so that neighbors believed she was unchaste, pregnant four or 5 weeks ago, that her father was her seducer, that Elizabeth provoked abortion by help of her father, mother, & Jane Ricknor, implying murder against Elizabeth. Those accusations have affected her spirits. She can never effectually surmount this matter, for female character once stained can never regain in estimation of mankind that purity which adorns innocence unsullied. Implores that Horton make amends. Wit: Daniel Ogden, Zechariah Smith

p.76
Buffaloe Dis^{t}, Natchez. 14 June 1797. Reubin Denham, Bayou Sarah Dis^{t}, planter, g^{dn} of dau Elizabeth, to Alcaldes Henry Hunter & Danl Clark, asks prosecution of Abr^{m} Horton for defamation of Elizabeth. Wit: Daniel Ogden, Zachariah Smith

Reubin Denham is advised to draw up and present the various charges against Abraham Horton at our next meeting, Saturday 17th ins^{t}. at Clarksville. Daniel Clark, H.Hunter, Alcaldes

Gov^{t} of Natchez, Dis^{t} of Buffaloe, 17 June 1797. Reubin Denham, Bayou Sarah, swears to Alcaldes H^{y} Hunter & Danl Clark that Abraham Horton invented and spread stories injurious to his character by insinuations that he debauched his daughter and caused her to destroy a child of which she was enceinte. In presence of Daniel Ogden, Zechariah Smith

District of Bayou Sarah. Barshuba Hunter swears that Sarah Horton & she went into Mr.Horton's peach orchard for peaches and heard some of Mr.Denhams family have ungenteel discourse but made no answer. They saw Denham come near the creek. He asked Sally to tell her father to come. Sally says, "What's that Mr.Denham, are you 'Looking Liberty.'" Mr.Denham asked again. Same reply. Jas.Horton told his father Denham wanted him. Horton went where Denham was, said, "What do you want?" Denham wished Horton to keep his children from blackguarding his (Denham's) children, that they could not work the field. Hugh Denham told Horton that they had tried to keep his cattle out of his field, and they could find powder & lead. Deponent saith that 3rd inst she heard a person from Horton's holler "Hang you" several times. Barshuba (X) Hunter
In presence of John Welton, E.Hunter

p.77
District of Bayou Sarah. Deposition of John (x) Parker: was at Abraham Horton's house on Sunday 3rd inst. Simon Hook or some of his company hollered to Deponent to bring over Mrs. Wimbush's hat and he would piss in it. Deponent, Nathan Horton & George Row went down to the creek. N.Horton told Hook to come over the creek if he wanted to fight. Hook answered he would not. Deponent asked Hook if Horton came over if he would clear him of the law. Hook replied he would, and would give him a blasted whipping. Deponent, N.Horton, & Geo. Row went over the creek on Denham's side. Abraham Horton said, "Denham, this is all your doings," and drew off his shirt. Denham said,"You are a blasted liar." Horton said it was not that Denham had been sending him challenges by every person that passed the house; that he could whip him. Horton told Denham that he was now on his side of the creek;if he wanted to fight he should have it as cheap as ever he had one. That it should not cost him one half bitt. Denham sd, "Blast you, I won't fight you." Mrs.Denham said,"Reubin, kill them all, you cannot be hurt for it." Horton answered, "I believe you have been pretty well used to killing," turned off and went home. Deponent heard someone say, "Daddy, here is your gun." Mrs.Ricknor said, "Run for God's sake or some of you will be killed." Further, Deponent says that he said he was the best man within two hundred yards of that place. John (x) Parker Henry Hunter. Benjamin Kimball. 23rd Sept 1797

pp.77-79
Dist Bayou Sarah. Nathan Horton's Deposition. Sunday evening 3rd inst, George Row and John Parker was at Abraham Horton's house, in the lane at play, heard a noise but could not tell what or where it was. Deponent, Row, and Parker went to the house. A person from Denham's plantation hollered to Parker & asked what they wanted. They said "Where is that speckled-faced Horton? I will whip him, G-- d him!" Parker answered. They said, "Bring Mrs.Wimbesh's hat here." Parker asked if they would p--s in it. They said,"Yes." Deponent, Row, and Parker went to the creek. Parker: "Here is the hat, if you will p--s in it as you said." They said they would not, but "If you are there, come over here & we will whip you." Parker: "You said you would whip that speckled-faced Horton, and if you are good to fight, come over & whip him." Denham:"Ah, you are there, Parker, you blasted S. of a B.! You had better be lying on Mrs.Wimbesh than be here." Parker said Denham would be glad if he had the chance to ly on her. Denham said, "Blast your heart, come over here and I'll slap your jaws. I am man enough for you."

All this while Deponent said nothing, but they knew he was there. Some of the party said they had an Idler for he said nothing; & asked where "Pidy" was, that speckled-faced ---, Horton. Deponent: "Here I am, what do you want?" Hook: "G--D-- you! If you are a man, come over here & I will whip you." Deponent, Rowe, & Parker advanced near creek bank. Deponent to Hook: "If you want to whip me, come here." Deponent said he was a stranger, and what did Hook want to fight him for? Hook: "You are a man, come over here, G--D-- you, I will whip you, G--D-- you!" One of Denham's boys said, "The first place we meet you we will whip you, & if one can't do it all, three can." Deponent said he never was beat by them until his bones was sore, and he did not want anything to do with them. It was Hook he wanted; he wants to whip me. Denham: "You little blasted S- of a B-, I will whip you, the first place I find you, & if you will come over here, blast your heart, I will whip you." Deponent:"Mr. Denham, I do not want anything to say to you, for it's Hook I want to see." With that there came a chunk. Someone, deponent believed in woods under first creek bank. Second chunk from same place. Deponent asked who was throwing chunks. No answer. Throwing fast as they could. Then: "Blast you, if you are men, come over here & we will whip you." Joseph Denham dared deponent to meet him half way on the log if he wouldn't come over.Deponent said he would; he had nothing against him, & he would shake hands with him. Denham met him on the creek bank. Then he turned and said, "God blast you, I will shake hands with you," & began throwing chunks fast as he could. Deponent returned to his company. Both sides throwing. Hook: "G-- D-- you, you are all cowards, for you run away. Come over here & I'll whip you, G-- D-- you." Deponent to his company, "Let's go and see if he will fight." We sot off. As we got to the log my father overtook us: "What is the matter?" Parker: "We are going to see if Hook will whip Nathan." Some of Denham's party said,"Here they come," and when we got on top the hill my father said "Here is a heap of them," and slipped off his shirt. Father: "Denham, this is all your contrivance; you have often said that you would whip us. If you want to whip me Mr.Denham, here I am." Deponent inquired for Hook, asked what he wanted to whip me for. My father: "Where is Hook? He has often sent challenges to my son. Let him come, he shall have fair play." Hook said he never sent a challenge. Denham: "Parker, you all hear, you blasted S-- of a B--." Parker said he was the best man within two hundred yards of this place. Denham said, "God blast your old soul; clear out, you blasted old S- of a B-." He seized a bayonet which his son Jos had in his hand, saying, "God blast his soul, I'll kill him," endeavoring to get bayonet from his son, but did not. Prior to this A.Horton went off home. Mrs.Denham said, "Kill them Reubin, for they all deserve to die." Denham let go the bayonet, turned as if going home. Someone said, "Daddy, here is your gun." Mrs.Ricknor: "Run, Horton, Denham has got his

gun. Run for God's sake, or he will kill you." Nathan Horton
In presence of John Hutton, E.Hunter 23 September 1797

p.79
Gov^{t} of Natchez, Dis^{t} Sandy Creek. Before Wm Cooper, one of his Majesty's Alcaldes, Mary Tanner swears she was at Abram Hortens and heard Horten order his children to go blackguard Reubin Denham's children. Horten's children went near where Denham's children was at work, & blackguarded Denham's children a considerable time. Denham came and told Sally Horten to tell her father to come talk with him. Sally used very ill language to Denham. After some time Horten came, & asked Denham what the devil he wanted. Denham said to keep his children from blackguarding his at their work. Horten said that he wouldn't do any such thing. Horten abused Denham and told Denham that as soon as Ricknor began making brandy he would come to the still-house & whip Denham,--he'd be damned if he didn't. Denham desired Horten to keep his children away from *his* when they were at work. Horten said he wouldn't & said as soon as they began to make brandy he would raise 4 or 5 young men and go whip Denham, his family, and tear down the still or the house. Deponeth further saith that on Saturday evening Wm Roach and his sister came to Denham. Sally Horten got up in a peach tree and called Wm Roach & told him that the heifer was there, & to "teach cows of the old bulls & if he went to the heifer the old bull would horn him, for the old bull had a stiff horn." Horten's family kept blackguarding Denham late in night, and Denham made no reply.
29 Sep^{t} 1797. Wit: William Lopez Mary Tanner

p.80
Bayou Sarah Dis^{t}. George Row's Deposition. He was at Abraham Horten's on Sunday third ins^{t} when a negro of Horten's told Nathan that Hook said he could whip him. Nathan called Hook at Denham's and asked if he wanted to whip him. Some person answered he would if he'd cross the creek. Nathan Horten,Jno Parker, & Deponent went down to the creek. Both sides used uncivil language. Jno Parker asked if they would "quit?" the law if they were to come over. Parker said to Nathan: "Let's see what they will do." John Parker, Nathan Horten, Abraham Horten, deponent and some of Mr. Horten's negroes went over. Reubin Denham ordered Horten and his company off his plantation. Abraham Horten replied, "You have said you would whip me and if you want to do it, now is the time." He stripped his shirt off. Reuben Denham said to his son, "Joseph, give me the bayonet, I will run him through." Joseph refused.Denham ordered them off again. Parker said he'd whip any man in 200 yards. Nathan asked Hook if he wanted to fight. Hook did not. Abraham & Nathan Horten, John Parker, & deponent went; as they crossed the creek Mrs.Ricknor hollered, "For God's

sake clear out, or he will kill some of you." Mrs. Denham said it would be no matter if he was to kill them all. Nathan Horten told Reubin Denham he wanted Hook. George Rowe

pp.80-81
Bayou Sarah Dis[t]. Simon Hook's deposition. Sunday night 3rd between 8 & 9 o'clock he heard hollering at Abraham Hortens. Reubin Denham asked if Indians were out; they believed not. Hook believes it to have been Nathan Horten calling loud for "Hang Jan," alluding to Reubin Denham, a fictitious name the Hortens called Denham, & at same time using profane, abusive language. Deponent went to still house at Conrad Ricknor's where Reubin's sons was. Abraham Horten, N.Horten, Jno Parker, and a white person and two Negroes Richard and Will came down the creek near the still house. Nathan Horten and John Parker insulted Denham's sons. Reuben Denham came where his sons and Deponent were, and told his sons to come, leave the fools. Abraham Horten's party threw clubs at Denhams. Denham, two sons left. Deponent said he wouldn't leave Hugh, & turned back. Jo[s] & W[m] Denham turned also. Nathan Horten or someone called, "Damn you, make ready, for we are coming over the creek." Jos. Denham called to his father that they were coming as Abraham Horten, Nathan Horten, John Parker, a white man, Richard, & Will came on top the ridge in Denham's plantation. Denham, sons, and deponent met them. Denham told Abraham Horten to go home and not disturb him in the dead of night. Abraham Horten replied he had come to whip Denham. He stripped off his shirt, but Denham did not choose to combat with him. John Parker said he could whip any man within two hundred yards. Nathan Horten offered to fight Joseph Denham, Joseph not agreeing. Denham again ordered Horten and company off his plantation. A.Horten replied it was not his plantation. Denham, a third time, told Horten to begone home, as did Mrs.Denham. Reubin Denham then got in a violent passion, seeking a weapon. Horton & party set off home & at some distance threw a club; an Indian from Denham's house was standing near was struck by it & hurt very much by it. Simon Hook Wit. Frederick Kimball and Zachariah Smith

p.82
Govt of Natchez, Bayou Sarah Dist. Reubin Denham's Deposition: Sunday night, 3rd inst., 8 or 9 o'clock, heard hollering, asked if Indians was out; believed not. Hollers continued. Deponent got out of bed, went to still house. Abraham Horten, son N.Horten, John Parker, unknown white person, two negroes (Horton's property) on other side of creek. Nathan Horten & John Parker cursed his sons, swore they would whip Denham boys, threw billets of wood across creek, which they returned. Deponent ordered sons to leave the fools and went, but son Hugh stayed. John Blackburn said he would not leave

Hugh, & Joseph & Wm Denham also went back. Some of Horton's company said, "Damn you, make ready, we are coming." Joseph Denham called his father. Deponent went where his sons were, on the creek bank in Deponent's plantation. Abraham Horten stripped and dared Deponent to fight; he ordered Horten off his plantation. Horten said it was not his plantation, & he would not go. He came to whip Deponent, & he'd be damned if he did not whip him or any man within two hundred yards. Deponent ordered all to begone. Abraham Horten said, "You are a damned old rascal, and I will whip you before I go." Deponent replied,"You had better begone or I will make you go" and ketched at a stick, but was prevented getting it by some of his family. Mrs.Denham told Horten to go,"or else you may get hurt." Nathan Horten, Jno Parker, the stranger, and Horten's negroes Richard & Will set off; after a small distance someone threw a club which struck an Indian that was looking on, and hurt him very bad. Deponent prays protection of law in bonding Abraham Horton, Nathan Horten, and Jno Parker for good behavior towards Deponent and his family, or injury to his property. 4th September 1797. Reubin [X] Denham
In presence of Zechariah Smith, Frederick Kimball

p.83
Bayou Sarah Dist. John Blackburn's Deposition. On Sunday he heard hollers. Reubin Denham asked if Indians were out. Deponent believes it was Nathan Horten hollering "Hang Jaw," & other aggravations. Abraham Horten, his son N. Horten, John Parker, another white person, and two negroes came to creek near still house. Nathan and John cursed Hugh, Joseph, Hugh, Wm Denham, swore they'd whip them, threw a club which struck deponent. Deponent had crossed the branch, & was standing on creek bank. Nathan and John kept throwing clubs which Denham boys returned. Denham told his sons to leave the fools. Deponent, Denham & sons Joseph & William set off. Hugh didn't. Deponent said he would not leave Hugh. He, Joseph & William turned back. Abraham Horten, N. Horten or John Parker said, "Damn you, make ready, for we are coming." Joseph called his father. Denham met them on the ridge. They had crossed creek in Denham's field. Denham told A. Horten to go and not disturb his family in the night. Horten said he would whip him and stripped off his shirt. J.Parker said he could whip any man within 200 yards. N.Horten offered to fight Joseph. Denham ordered them off his plantation. A.Horten said it wasn't his plantation, & he would whip him. Denham again, "Horten, you had better go home." Mrs.Denham said to Horten, "You had better go home or you may get hurt." Denham got in a violent passion. Horten and party crossed the creek to go home. Some of his party threw a club and struck an Indian, and hurt him very bad. John Blackburn
Sworn 4th day of September 1797. H.Hunter, Alcalde

p.84
Bayou Sarah Dist. Deposition of Daniel McConnell. At Mr.Denham's house, 6 or 7 weeks ago, in the night he heard Nathan Horten holler "Oh Hang Jaw" several times, "take care of the young heifer for the young bulls was coming" & "Its Liberty I want" and further saith not. Sworn to before me H. Hunter, Alcalde. In presence of John Welton, E. Hunter

Bayou Sarah District. Deposition of John Hilton. He went to house of Abraham Horten by request of Henry Hunter, Esq., to see cattle supposed to be shot. Deponent saith he found him to be shot with a small shot. Deponent further heard Abraham Horten say he would invite neighbors to go to Ricknors soon as he made brandy and drink it, for he owed him money, & he knew of no other way to get it. Some person replied maybe he would let you have it. Horten said, "Then I will duck him."
4th October 1797 John Hilton

Bayou Sarah Dist. 23 Sept 1797. Deposition of Jno Row.
At Reubin Denham's house, Denham told him he wished the Horten family would let his family alone at their work. Denham desired deponent to tell Horten the same; Deponent saith he did, and further saith not. John Row
Sworn to before me, this 23rd of September 1797. H. Hunter

p.85
Deed. Richard Goodwin of Province of Louisiana, District of Natchez, to St.Germain. Six Hundred Dollars to be paid first March next; 600 acres surveyed by Wm Vousdan for sd Goodwin, joining lands of sd St.Germain, other sides vacant. Also to St. Germain one-third part of the saw mill on sd plantation, reserving to his own use house, plantation, conveniences belonging to it untill ensuing crop be sold to best advantage. St. Germain is to possess his third part of saw mill at his pleasure. 23 March 1785. Richard Goodwin
H. Marmaduke, witness

Received Mr.St.Germain's note for one Hundred Sixty Dollars which is to furnish me a security in full of all amounts except Eighty odd Dollars which is under arbitration. Natchez, 28th February 1785, on account of our dispute on partnership of the plantation or other affairs except as above. Nehemiah Alberts. Witness: William Smith, John Short

Peter Hawkins to St.Germain, Negro Hannah, Four Hundred Dollars, warranted from all manner of claims. 21 October 1784, Natchez. Peter Hawkins

p.86

I give St.Germain all horses he can find here or in the Nation branded "N on T.C" belonging to the Hawkins and Nation, to satisfy all amounts he has against Hawkins & Nation.
Oct. 21, 1784 Peter Hawkins

Deed, John Tenisen to St. Germain, Six Hundred Dollars paid by St.Germain, sold Negro man named Baker, which sd Negro is warranted from all manner of claims. John [x] Tenison
August 18th 1784. Natchez

Deed, Nehemiah Albertson to St. Germain, for Three Hundred Dollars, Negro William, warranted from all manner of claims.
4 December 1783. Nehemiah Albertson

pp.86-89 GOVERNMENT ORDER

Governor Manuel Gayoso De Lemos, recognizing need for proper pens for cattle & horses, under regulations to protect stock against ravages of wild beats and also to guard against the inconveniences that attend the making of Indigo, grants the following ordinance. Pens shall be made eighty feet by forty with proper posts and bars. To be erected: one by J.Gaillard and A. Ellis, one by Saml. Hutchins and I.H.White, one by D. Williams and I. Lintott, one by R. Bacon and & N. Tomlinson, one by R.Swayze & P.Shillin, one by D.Grafton and I.Bernard, one by C. Boardman and W. Pipes, one by James Bonner and T. Jordan, one by A.Beale and J.Girault, one by I.Lum & N.Ivy, one by A. & I.Henderson, one by J.Calvit and B.Belk, one by Jer.Coleman and I.Foster, one by R.King and B.Curtis, one by I.Johnson & R.Ford, one by S.Heady and I.Oglesby, one by I. Armstreet and T.Morgan, one by J.Minor and S.Holmes, one by A.Scanlin and C.King, one by P.Presler and I.Carter.

Appoints in District of Villa Gayoso William Murray and John Smith, Esq., to point out most convenient places to erect pens. For same purpose on Bayou Pierre, appoints Col. Peter Bruin and Mr. William Brocas, on Big Black, Messrs. G. Rapalji and Tobias Brocas, on south side Homochitto, Messrs. James Nicholson & Ruffin Gray, at Buffalo Charles Percy Esq, and on Bayou Sarah Francis Raupeto and John Hunter, Esq, sd pens under same regulations as those above expressed.

[Ordinance continues rules for use, exact dimensions of fences, bounty on wolf and tiger scalps, rules for making Indigo so as not to injure water supply, hunting licenses.]

Appoints Ezekiel Forman treasurer of funds from sale of stray animals and rewards for killing beasts of prey.

Natchez. 1 February 1793 Manuel Gayoso de Lemos

His Lordship from Stephen Miro, New Orleans; introduces Don William Conway of N.O., who wishes a grant in order to form a settlement at [blank] Creek. Surveyor General is to establish the acreage and Miro sets the terms.

p.90
Chas Trudeau certificate for Wm Conway [blank] acres, superficial measures of Paris, situated on the river, certificate conforms to plat by Wm Vousdan, surveyor for Natchez Dist.

Solomon Whetley's petition for 400 arpents on Bayou Pierre, bounded by land of John Booker. Natchez, 12th April 1790.

Order from Stephen Miro to Surveyor of Province, Don Charles Laveau Trudeau to locate and establish in favor of the above four hundred arpents of land square measure if vacant, without causing injury to any person, and keeping his roads and bridges in good repair, within term of one year. Settle same within three years.

William Dunbar, Deputy Surveyor, certifies he surveyed 400 arpents land to Solomon Wheetley between Homochitto about 25 miles E N E from Fort Panmure. 25 November 1797

p.91
At Fort Panmure of Natchez on 22 February 1787 Comdt Chas De Grand Pre learned from planter Hy Marmadue that James Brown had died in his house without leaving a will & sd Marmadue's inventory of Brown's possessions: plantation on a branch of Fairchild Creek. On 28 February De Grand Pre orders plantation valued and sold; has empowered Henry Marmadue and David Tanner to complete same; land is valued at 80 Dollars. Witnesses: Philander Smith, J Vaucheri, Barchelot Des Hubles, Thos Henderson

Mississippi Territory, Adams County. Certification by Eben Kees, Translator and keeper of the Spanish Records, that he translated from Spanish a grant of 400 arpents made out to Solomon Whitley. 20th January 1816

Undated request from Edn Randolph that an enclosed patent be translated and sent back to him by Colling's return.

p.93 [There is no p.92 in the typed book.]
Natchez, 12 Decr 1785 certification by James Jackson that in past year he was overlooker of James Elliot's plantation and slaves at Coles Creek. Last winter Elliot brought home Negro "True Blue" who was sick on arrival, had a lengthy illness & died last fall.

Natchez, 12 March 1785, Bill of Sale, Sutton Banks to James Elliot, Negro "True Blue," warranted for one year, 450 Dollars. Witness: William Gilbert

p.93-94
Will of Tacitus Gaillard, Natchez Dist. Has already advanced shares to son Isaac Gaillard and to daughters Ann Savage and Elizabeth Farar. Bequest to dau Elizabeth Farar's children. To dau Margaret Gaillard ten Negro slaves equal to one fifth of my slaves, to grand-niece Elizabeth Gaillard young Negro wench. Remainder, real and personal, to wife Ann Gaillard. Executors wife Ann, Ann Savage, Margaret Gaillard, son Isaac Gaillard. 29 July 1785. Witness Jesse Carter, Richard Ellis, John Ellis, John Eldergill, Archibald Palmer.

p.94-95
25 Novr 1752 Tacitus Gaillard of Charlestown to John Gendron Junr of Santee. Ann Gaillard wife of Tacitus formerly Ann le Grand, inheritance of 480 acres, her 1/3 part of tract of 1406 acres lying at Trembay near Santee River in Craven Co., exchanged with her husband her land for 14 good negro slaves by lease and release 1 and 2 June 1749. Tacitus sold the 480 acres to Jno Mayrant. Now Tacitus sells to Jno Gendron Junr the 14 slaves: Hester, Cezar, Cane, Zaripa, Joan, Jucs, Hazar, Susy, George, Jemmy, Johnny, Dick, Daniel, and Frank. Wit: Edward Serman, John Desseline

p.95-97
19 Augt 1783. John Mayrant to Charles Contoy both of Craven County, SC. Mayrant had loaned the slaves to Tacitus, not subject to his debts, and at his death to be divided 1/3 to his wife, & remainder equally among his living children. Jno Mayrant now sells to Charles Contoy slaves Juba, Elsey, Fortune, Harriette, Esther, Frank, Susie, Charles, Espenel Hattey, Prince, & Dottey; permits s^{d} Tacitus to use said slaves during his life for $2250. Witness: Wm Bell, J. Mayrant.
28 February 1785, William Bell proves above deed before Danl Florry, one of His Majestie's Justices for Craven County. Recorded in Book MM page 468.

p.98
Lanius [D.P.] Peary certifies that when he left Natchez for New Orleans on 13 November 1784 with his passport on board, Mr.Treaveaner forbid him to take Mrs.Woods into his boat except at White Cliffs. Mr. Minor was interpreter.
Jesse Hamilton certifies he heard above words spoken by Mr. Minor to Mr. Peary. Natchez, February 23, 1786.

Stephen Jett's Certificate, 4 Oc^{t} 1784: Proposals by Captain John Woods for the payment of his contract with Steven Minor on Minor's making good the deficiencies in s^{d} contract, viz: quantity of land contracted for, legal titles to lands. Also deficiencies of 34 bushels of corn, 1 cow and calf, 1 plough and fixing. Capt Woods gave Mr. Minor two notes of hand, one for one Thousand Dollars payable 25 December 1783, the other for five hundred Dollars payable 1 May following. Minor refused to sign or make title, but Woods had to pay his bonds. When first note came due Minor sent constable and guard, and took possession of Capt Woods negroes: 1 fellow, 2 wenches & 2 children; had them conveyed to the fort. Commandant gave Mrs.Woods, wife of Capt.John Woods, her choice of one of the negro wenches with her child, the other three remained still in the possession of Stephen Minor. Stephen Jett

1 October 1784. Stephen Jett certifies that Negro woman Kate was property of Mrs.Margaret Woods wife of John Woods, given to Margaret by her father Mathew Thompson at her marriage to John Woods, and that promised Margaret that he, John, would never sell or dispose of sd woman Kate to any person without leave of her, Margaret Woods. Archibald Lea, Stephen Jett

Natchez Dis^{t}, 1 Oc^{t} 1784. Archibald Lea certifies he heard Capt John Woods 12 years ago make gift to his wife Margaret of Negro Rebekah, age then about 8 years; John Woods divested himself of any title whatsoever to s^{d} girl. John promised Margaret that he would never dispose of Rebekah without consent of Margaret. Lea frequently heard him say that he had no right to Rebekah; she was property of Margaret Woods.

p.100
5 April 1786. Order: Marquis de Sonora to Count de Galvez, Capt Genl of Two Floridas, concerns inconveniences noted by Stephen Miro, Gov.of La., that would result from attempts to remove English and American families now settled in Baton Rouge, Mobile, Pensacola, & Natchez out of s^{d} provinces, and directing that families who stay must swear Duty to his Majesty. Those who do not agree are to go to North American colonies. Irish clergymen will serve those who remain.

p.101
Agreement betwixt John Stilly and James Brown, provides that George and William Holloway or two others as good shall work in the crop along with four able negroes. 30 April 1785

Stephen Haywood says that corn from Capt James Elliott that Haywood was told by Benjamin Farar 18th May 1786 to receive, was damaged. Haywood thought it improper to receive s^{d} corn.

p.101-102
Petition of Abner Green: his dispute with James Elliott re-

specting a flat sold and delivered to sd Elliott. Appeals to Gov. Miro for redress. Natchez, August 2, 1786

p.102
John Smith declares that he was with Abner Green when he was repairing a flat since sold to James Elliott. Suspicious she was rotten, Smith took a chisel, examined her, and found her sound, clean and dry. Elliott refused to accept the flat and corn. On 20 March Smith was with Green and Elliott. Elliott wanted flat examined by two men and a certificate given. Mr. Green chose Earl Douglas and Mr. Elliott chose Smith. They found flat strong, tight, and sufficient to carry her load according to her certificate dated 25 March 1786. Smith told Elliott if flat was not immediately loaded she would shrink, should be filled with water to swell her plank. Smith later saw her loaded and 18 or 20 inches deeper at one end. A boat 42 feet long, 8 feet wide & loaded in such manner caused her joints to open. The Person in charge said he was ordered so to do by Elliott. Some time later Smith heard that the flat began to leak, believes not from careless building, but from uncommon way of loading, shrinking of plank, or accident. On 13 May Grand Pre ordered Smith, Mr.Douglas & 3 others to examine the flat. Was surprised to see part of her sides split out, head and stern abused. Natchez, 6 August 1786

p.103-104
Natchez, 7 August 1786. Declaration of William [x] Nowlin. After Abner Green sold James Elliott the flat, Nowlin several times delivered corn on board. James Edward complained Mr Elliott his employer did not give him assistance respecting management of the flat, over 800 bushels corn aboard, could not give her necessary attention. Nowlin recommended to Elliott that he put a pump aboard. Elliott said flat and cargo weres for Dr Farar. Examined by John Smith and Earl Douglas: leakage was probably because of shrinkage of planks after having lain dry too long after she was calked.

p.104-105
Natchez, 7 August 1786 James [x] Edwards declaration. He was employed by James Elliott to attend a flat sold him by Abner Green, and to receive corn on board. He saw Elliott, Green & one of his negroes bringing the flat up the creek. They said she was taken by a fresh in the creek, they found her lodged against 2 trees. Edwards had long acquaintance with loading flats, thinks leak was caused by shrinkage of upper planks. Edwards could have stopped every leak, but Elliott continued putting in corn as fast as it could be brought, Edwards had no time to attend the leaks.

p.105

Caleb King's Declaration. By Commandant's order he inspected a flat sold by Abner Green to James Elliott. Believed her to have lain dry too long dry and her planks had shrunk. Abner Green asked Elliott to show him the rotten parts of which he had complained to the Commandant; Elliott said he knew of no such place. About a fortnight ago Elliott said flat was supposed to carry 6 or 700 bushels of corn; he had put on board 1010 bushels; upwards of 50 bushels was spoiled by leakage.

p.106
24 Au^{g} 1786. Thomas [x] Calvit Declares that on Tuesday 8th Abner Green asked Douglas to certify the condition of a flat in dispute between Green and Elliott at the time she was examined by order of Commandante. Douglas replied he had given 2 certificates about sd flat which contradicted each other; that he would appear a vile rascal, but the flat had not the same appearance at last examination as upon the first; that he believed she had been much abused. If a pump had been on board, she was sufficient to carry the load.

27 Jul 1786. John [x] Terry certifies that the Comdt ordered Elliott to receive his corn. Mr.Minor had taken upon himself to have the flat loaded for Mr.Farar. Elliott would be able to receive Terry's corn in a few days.

Natchez Dist. Cato West certifies that early in January last he was present when James Elliott purchased of Abner Green a flat now in dispute, and also corn and pork, to be delivered 10th February or as soon as flat could be launched. Believes Elliott received neither till late March, Dr.Farar not sending to receive flat and corn which were for him.

p.107
Coles Creek, 25 March 1786. John Smith and Earl Douglas chosen by James Elliott & Abner Green to examine the boat which they find sufficient to load with greatest safety.

Natchez, 27 May 1786. Richard Duval states that he examined a flat, property of Abner Green, and found her insufficient to carry her burden of corn.

Natchez, 27 [no month] 1786. Andrew Rendall certifies that the flat was not sufficient to carry a load.

Natchez, 23 May 1786. D.W.Coughlin declares the flat was not fit for any service.

p.108.
Natchez, 27 May 1786. Earl Douglas states he was deceived in first examination of the flat built by Green for Elliott. At

second examination she was not capable of carrying a load.

26 May 1786. Wm Geoghegan declares he assisted James Elliott in bailing water out of a flat. Two negroes helped "They and me the whole night were employed busily in throwing out water and endeavoring to stop leaks in the flat; in the night both her bulkheads fell out notwithstanding every effort myself & the two negroes could make to the contrary, she sunk a foot in the night, the water coming in almost in every part of the flat."

p.108-109
Coles Creek, 29 May 1786. William [x] Nowland certifies he took a cartload of corn for Mr.West to be put on board the flat built by Abner Green. A mulatto man was laboring very hard at bailing out water. He appearing much fatigued, Nowland took the bucket to relieve him, Nowland threw out water as fast as he could for about half hour. The man took bucket again, and we continued bailing by turns until Elliott came from John Smith's farm 4 miles from where the flat lay. Next day, the flat unloaded, Nowland looked her over and thought she would sink entirely before night.

17 May 1786. Caleb King certifies that when ordered by Com^{dt} he viewed Elliott's flat at Boyd's Creek, and is of opinion she is unfit for service, being much shrunk by lying dry.

Natchez, 27 May 1786. J.Duncan certifies the flat he was ordered by Comdt to view was unfit for service.

Natchez Dist, 3 June 1786. Wm Vousdan & Lewis Chachere, arbitrators chosen to settle dispute between James Elliott and Abner Green find we cannot agree; refer same to an umpire.

p.110
11 August 1786. Wm [x] Richardson declares he was employed by James Elliott last April to take care of corn from a flat repaired & sold by Abner Green, corn said to have been taken out because the flat's rotten bottom leaked. In the 3 weeks Richardson was there she did not leak two gallons. About 50 bushels corn damaged by rain was throwed into Richard Devals with undamaged corn.

Natchez, 11 Sep^{t} 1786. Nehemiah [x] Martin certifies he saw Abner Green take care to have work done well when he was repairing flat he sold James Elliott. Later Martin assisted in taking from her bottom damaged corn layed there to dry & put it aboard Richard Devals flat with undamaged corn. The flat Elliott had did not appear to leak any.

p.110-111
Opinion of Wm Vousdan, arbitrator at desire of Abner Green & James Elliott and acceded to by Colonel Grand Pre. Green has acted judiciously. Flat had been carried by a fresh in Coles Creek where, jammed between trees, it may have received damage. Elliott's orders about loading caused damage. Elliott can have no claim against Green.

p.111-112
Natchez, 3 August 1786. Bill/Sale Stephen Holston, for 400 Dollars paid by Mary Higdon, both of Natchez Dis^{t}, Province of Louisiana. Negro woman Rose. Witness: John Bolls

p.112
Letter from D.Smith informing [name not stated] that 500 men and party of Indians are embarking for this Post under Capt. Davenport, depending upon s^{d} Smith for ammunition; he needs supplies from addressee; expects to see the American colors flying in Natchez Fort. Genl Green successful against Cherokees and Creeks. July 25, 1786

Natchez, 25 Sep^{t} 1785. Agreement between Stephen Jordan and his son Thomas Jordan. Stephen conveys his real and personal property except 2 cows and calves, 2 sows and litter, 1 gray mare, his own bald faced horse, some tools. Thomas agrees to build a house wherever Stephen may chuse, to furnish Stephen with board, lodging, washing, mending. Thomas to pay Stephen 200 Dollars & 600 lbs meat yearly, Stephen to have ½ household furniture. Thomas to pay Stephen's debts contracted before this date. Witness: Daniel Grafton, Robert Dunbar

Natchez, 21 October 1786. Arbitrators chosen by Stephen Jordan and his son Thomas Jordan are of opinion that to prevent further altercations Thomas Jordan is to give up everything upon the plantation, his own furniture and clothes excepted, to Stephen Jordan, and that Stephen pay him 500 Dollars. Sutton Bankes. Caleb King.

21 October 1785. Petition of Anthony Hutchins to Commandant. Patience Coleman, widow of Wm Coleman, indebted to John Farquhar 139 Dollars seven Ryals of which greatest part was due from Coleman estate. After she married Immanuel Madden the memorialist, to prevent a suit, at request of Patience, paid Farquhar afsd sum & took note for same from sd Immanuel, her husband. Patience hath since eloped from Immanuel, married a Kentucky man, hath not paid debt nor hath Emanuel property to discharge debt; yet hath assets left by deceased; memorialist prays he may be paid out of same.

p.113-114

Inhabitants of Natchez Dis^{t} assembled 4th ins^{t} & elected and app^{td} the subscribers to cross Mississippi R at Fort Panmure to examine cattle which arrived 20 days ago from Attakapaws. They found no distemper. Stephen Howard, had care of s^{d} cattle, stated on oath no distemper amongst them. Natchez 7 Nov 1786. C.Bingaman, Sam O.Gibson, John Bisland, Jacob Cobun

19 Novr 1789. Immanuel Madden promises to pay Anthony Hutchins on order 139 Dollars 7 bits. Manuel [x] Madden

p.115
Constantino McKenna's certification that in October 1788, at request of Jno Girault, he visited Lainneville LeDuc who was having convulsions. McKenna administered Extreme Unction.LeDuc died about eight o'clock that evening. Next day McKenna and Mr.White officiated at Lainneville LeDuc's funeral.
15 July 1790. Constantino McKenna

Gregory White's certification that he had officiated at the funeral of Lainneville LeDuc. Natchez, 15 July 1790

Subscribers certify they were personally acquainted with Mr. Lainneville LeDuc. The coffin being not quite finished when the company arrived, he was put into it with the subscribers help. They uncovered LeDuc's face, examined him, and saw him nailed up, and carried three miles to the cemetery where he was interred, clergy attending. Natchez, 15 July 1790
Sam P. Moore, Wm McIntosh, Wetling Wootley[Melling Woolley?]

William Vousdan certifies he was personally acquainted with Lainneville LeDuc when he resided with John Girault, that he directed a person to Dr.Flowers to attend LeDuc; Vousdan arrived at funeral before the coffin was finished, and helped to put LeDuc into it. Reports that LeDuc is alive are false. Natchez, 15 July 1790.

p.115-116
Proclamation by Francis Lewis El Baron de Carondelet warning inhabitants of Natchez against insubordination. New Orleans, 24 May 1797. Copy by Andres Lopez Armento, Natchez, 3 June 1797.

p.117
Proclamation. Only Roman Catholic families employed in agriculture or mechanical arts are to be admitted to settle this province and West Florida. No rowers, hunters,Indian traders or vagabonds of the woods, without religion or subordination are to be admitted. New Orleans, 18th August 1783. By order of Stephen Miro. Signed Philipe Trevino

p.117-118
Proclamation by Louis, King of France, against persons stirring up troubles and threatening the peace of the kingdom. Versailles, 9 August 1789.

p.118
Unsigned, undated letter to Alexander Baillie requesting him to take charge of the writer's business while he is absent.

p.119
Deposition by William [W.N.] Nubeary, 22 Octr 1787: Before Isiril Folsom left this nation to go to the Natchez, Nubeary bought 18 cattle from him for five horses & $80 cash. Folsom gave the horses and cash to his son Nathaniel for negro boy Peter. Nathaniel Folsom delivered sd horses to Mr.Turnbull in the Chickasaw Nation. Witness: Henry [x] Dukes

Deposition by Thomas Hamilton, Natchez, 20 November 1787. He heard Nathaniel Folsom say that boy Peter, formerly property of his dec^{d} father, belongs to his younger brother Edmond.

Deposition of Daniel Whitaker, Natchez, 1787. Whitaker says while he lived at Mr. Welch's, Welch had hired the negro boy Peter, who was called old Folsom's property.

9 Octr 1797 John [x] Honler certified-- Before Israel Folsom left this Nation to go to the Natchez to purchase boy Peter for his son Nathaniel Folsom for which he sold cattle to Wm Newberry, half breed Chickasaw Indian, for horses and cash, which Israel Folsom paid to Nathaniel Folsom for afsd negro in Chickasaw Nation. Israel Folsom sent negro to Chickasaws by Nathaniel Folsom and desired him to keep him.

pp.119-120
Letter [name and date illegible] "Dare Brother....Don't you no that the negor boy that beelonged to our father that is deceast, he sold him to Samuel Jones, and my Deare Brother, you no that that negro beelonged to Robert Wade. Before you left the Nation that hee never was the property of my father in this world...."

p.120
Deposition of D. Holt, 20 Septr 1786. Holt was with Israel Folsom, decd, 2 or 3 days before he died, wrote his will and was a witness to same. He was in sound memory. Bequeathed to his son Esmund Folsom a negro Peter, which he had left with his son Nathaniel Folsom in Chickasaw Nation. Holt observed that perhaps son Nathaniel would not give Peter up as he was called a great sharper. The Deceased had lived a neighbor to Holt about two years. Witness: Cato West

Deposition of Peter Hawkins. Certifies he was living in the Chickasaw when Israel Foulsom arrived; During the considerable time Israel lived there, Hawkins never heard him claim a negro as his property.

Deposition of Anthony [--]. He was in Chickasaw Nation last April at Benjamin Jamison's, near Robert Wade's, where negro Peter was living with an Indian wench formerly kept by Wade, & was informed by Benj[n] Jamison he was left to pay a debt in case Robert Wade did not return at a certain time; Nathaniel Folsom was his attorney. Robert Welch told Anthony the negro was formerly his property; he had sold him to Robert Wade.

p.120-121
Deed, 3 August 1786. Nathaniel Folsom to James Wilson negro fellow named Peter. Witness: Samuel Jones, Jesey [x] Edwards

p.121
Will of Israel Foulson of Natchez District, West Florida. To son Edmund, negro Peter I left in Choctaw Nation with my son Nathaniel. Two daughters Salley and Abagale, cows and mares, some in Choctaw Nation, except horse named Noble, to son Edmund, also two yoke of oxen and two heifers that I bought of Captain Crane, not yet delivered. Executor & Guardian to my children Thomas Murdock. 23 November 1784
Attest: Thomas M.Green, Jacob Stampley, D.Holt

Deposition of Cato West, Natchez Dist. 20 Sept 1786. Soon after Israel Folsom arrived in this District, Cato heard him say he left negro Peter in the Indian Nation. Folsom lived about two years neighbor to Cato, behaved as an honest man.

p.122
Deposition of Berry James. 30 Oct[r] 1786. Never knew Israel Folsom, dec[d], ever owned negro man in dispute between James Wilson of the Natchez and Folsom of Natchez District. Knew sd negro since he was brought to this nation by John Whitehead. Wit: Jemillo Jones, Austin Sartors.

Deposition of Robert Welch, first owner of negro Peter; knew every master Peter had in this Nation; he never belonged nor ever was property of Mr. Folsom, late of Natchez, deceased.

Deposition of William Tholings. 3 Feb.1788. Four or five y[rs] ago Tholings lived at William Newberry's house in Chickasaw Nation, when Israel Folsom & son Nathaniel lived in Chickasaw. Israel Folsom bought of his son Nathaniel the negro boy Peter for payment of which Israel sold Wm Newberry some cattle for horses; Israel delivered sd horses to son Nathaniel,

also eighty or ninety dollars. Tholings said to the old man: "You have a likely negro fellow now?" He said "Yes," that a negro suited him best in his old age, & that he had paid his son for him in horses and money which suited his son.
Witness: I Ferguson, James Smith

Deposition of Nathan Folsom. The negro man named Peter that he sold James Wilson of Natchez District never was the property of Israel Folsom deceased, that he never possessed said negro, that the negro is property of James Wilson.

p.123
Deposition of Alex.Fraser. 5 Novr 1786. James Wilson asked Fraser concerning the negro he bought of Nathaniel Folsom of Choctaw Nation, which negro was formerly property of Robert Wade, trader of this Nation, which negro sd Wade told Folsom to sell if he never returned from Virginia to pay debt contracted between them to Swanson McGillvray & Co. Thinks old Folsom never had a negro in this Nation.

Deposition of Thomas M.Green. Natchez District. 20 September 1786. Was at Israel Folsom's 2 or 3 days before he died; saw him sign the will he saw in Jesy Briant's possession; he appeared sound in memory & senses. Folsom bequeathed to Edmond Folsom negro Peter which he had left in Choctaw Nation with son Nat Folsom; desired Murdock, guardian to Folsom's children, to get sd negro soon as possible. Deceased was neighbor to Green about two years and behaved as an honest man.

Richard Devall to Grand Pre; execution is levied on Devall's property in consequence of a mortgage he gave James Mather. Devall will deliver an inventory; seeks to prevent additonal expense to the large sum he now faces. [no date]

p.124-125
Ezekial Duet and Henry Marmadue, arbitrators betwixt George Bailey agt Sutton Banks, with evidence of James Kelly, find that Bailey left Banks employ without provocation. Banks to pay 20 Dollars to Bailey; the 20 to be deducted from a debt Banks paid to estate of Richard Carpenter decd. 26 May 1789.

p.124
Will of Joseph Forrester, of Natchez Dis^{t} & Ireland. To the daughter of Pattey McKey, dec^{d}, formerly at Jacob's Cr^{k} near Crossing Place within about 42 miles of Fort Pitt, her child aged about 15 years, all property, personal and real, after debts &c paid. Caleb and Justus King extrs. 10 July 1787, New Orleans. Witness: William Smith, Robert Scage, Wm Coxon

Agreement Stephen Jorden with John Wilton, John and Wm Coalman, all Natchez Dist. Jorden rents plantation he lives on from 5 Feb[y] 1787 with 2 horses, 2 plows, 2 gears, 7 sows, 35 pigs, 100 bushels corn and for 6 wks a negro man. Colemans & Wilton to provide 6 hands, to fence from house to creek, and to give Stephen Jorden 1/3 the corn, tobacco, oats, return horses, plows, gears, sows, ½ the pigs with ½ the increase. 3 February 1787. Witness William Cooper, D. Smith

p.125
To end the affairs of John Stilles, absconded, three persons who have not had yet any connections which might hinder them in settling difficulties arising between interested parties, James Kirk, Peter Walker, Eben Wilkens are to examine books & accounts of John Stilles, hear witnesses, take oaths, and determine every particular in litigation. To defend the absent party, George Fitzgerald. Debtors mentioned in Stilles' books must present themselves before the gentlemen, who will meet in Mr. Vouchere's house every weekday except Saturday to begin Monday the 21st of this month until the 1st of June inclusive. May 1787. Carlos de Grand Pre.

p.126
John Short, appointed by the Trustees to the Estate of late Manuel and Benjamin Monsanto, for collecting debts due to sd Estate in the Natchez, as appears by deed filed in Notary's office, New Orleans, Received of Richard Bacon four Hundred Twelve Dollars, full amount of the obligation with legal interest thereon. Obligation cancelled; Richard Bacon is released. Natchez. 10 November 1789. John Short
Witness: John Girault, John Cornes, Thomas Tyler

p.127
Natchez Dist. Stephen Jordan's will. Grandson Wm Jordan my plantation, 2 largest plows, John Carmack's bond, agreement with Evan Shelby for 145£ VA currency in hands of W[m] Cock in Virginia, hogs, salt pork, horse, saddle, bridle, utensils, sled, double trees. To son Thomas Jordan cart, gears. Granddaughter Peggy Jordan, bed, bedstead, bedding, hat racks. To Mollie Grafton largest table and best half pewter, remainder to her dau Elizabeth Grafton. To Thomas Grafton brown mare & increase, small plough. Negro Dick his freedom. 18 January 1788. Executors John Bisland, Daniel Grafton. Witness: John Short, John Wilton, Johnnie [x] Holston, Moses [x] Bonner, Jacob Liestard, William Foster

p.127-128
Will of Uslah [x] Simmons. To son James Simmons, Negro boy Aberdeen, ½ cattle of late husband James Simmons, ½ hogs and horses, reserving 1 cow, 1 horse, 1 bed, ½ household furniture. To son Jacob Simmons, plantation, other ½ of cattle,

hogs, horses. Son Charles Simmons executor. 10 July 1788. Witnesses John Stowers, Joseph Bonner, William Collins

p.128
State of North Carolina, Davidson County. 11 April 1788. Adams Hampton agt Geo.Cook. John Walters' deposition: He purchased of Geo.Cook land in afsd county. Cook made him right to same, by assigning over to him a bond on Benjamin Drake, original proprietor; he paid Cook in full for same. On trial Hampton agt Cook it appeared by testimony of witnesses that George Cook had before sold same land to said Adams Hampton and had given him a bond to make title to same.
Thos.Molloy, Elijah Robertson, justices of sd court.

p.128-129
George Cooke, Davidson County, No.Carolina, bound unto John Sutton, Sumner County, No.Carolina, 400 pounds lawful money of this State, 18 July 1787, condition that if George Cooke make lawful right to part of a tract of land lying on South Fork Whites Creek, all on North side sd Creek to Jno Sutton, as soon as Cooke shall obtain a right; this obligation to be void, else to remain in force. To which was marked name Ge° Cooke with William Hooper, Absalom Hooper witnesses. On back of obligation was assignment of within bond to Adams Hampton without recourse to Sutton for value received, 23 Sept.1787. Marked John Sutton. Thomas Hampton and John Greggs, witnesses thereto. A true copy. Andrew Ewing.

p.129
Andrew Ewing of Davidson County certified that Cooke sold above lands to John Walker, who made oath of same; judgment given against sd Cooke was in consequence of above bond.

Power/Attorney, Adam Hampton of Davidson County, No.Carolina to Christopher Lightholder of same, to demand and recover of George Cooke a judgment of Four Hundred Pounds & costs which I recovered by attachment against him, Davidson County Court 10 April 1788. 25 April 1788. Wit.: J. Robertson

Acknowledgment by Adam Hampton before Justice James Robertson, Davidson County, No.Carolina, that above Power/Attorney is his act for purposes therein mentioned. 25 April 1788
p.130
Certification of James Robertson by Andrew Ewing with seal of Davidson County, 25 April 1788.

Deposition of Samuel Bell: Understands Drake sold 640 acres White's Creek to George Cooke, giving Cooke his bond to make rights to tract as soon as rights returned from the office. Ge° Cooke sold North part of s[d] tract to Sutton, giving him his obligation to make his rights to it as soon as he should obtain them from Drake, which obligation Hampton bought from Sutton. Major Hampton asked Ge° Cooke if he intended leaving without making him rights to s^d land; Cooke assured him that he would make him rights. To my certain knowledge s^d Cooke had sold af^sd bond on Drake to John Walker.

Davidson County Court, 10 April 1788. Adams Hampton against George Cook. Attachment. Jury found for plaintiff damages £400, Costs of suit expended 2.2d.
Certification by Andrew Ewing, Clerk of Davidson County, the above is a true transcript from record. 14 April 1788.

p.131
Daniel Clark, New Orleans, 20 August 1788, to Governor Miro. Examined the Demand of Christopher Lightholder, attorney for Adam Hampton against George Cook, Natchez District. Suggests Cook be allowed one year to appeal the judgment at Nashville or to pay the judgment, giving security in the interim.

A. Strothers & Daniel Clark, New Orleans, 20 August 1788, to Gov.Miro. Demand of Christopher Lightholder ag^t Jn° Montgomery & Joseph Calvet, Natchez District. Opinion that Montgomery and Calvit pay Lightholder for 1305 pounds sugar at 12 shillings Nashville money per pound, with interest from Novr 1787 untill paid in silver Mexican Dollars according to current value. Montgomery and Calvet to give security.

p.131-132
Alex^r Moore and Peter Walker, app^td by Com^dt De Grand Pre to settle between John Farquhar and Samuel Rayner respecting a note given by former to latter. Opinion: Farquhar paid 366 Dollars 7 bitts, leaving overpayment of 16 Dollars 7 bitts. Natchez Landing. 9 February 1788.

p.132
Will of Christopher Lightholder, Davidson County, No.Carolina. Estate to Methodist Church. Executors Headon Wells & Mr. Dennon. 8 May 1788. Test: Oliver Williams, Acquila Carmick. Certification of above will by Andrew Ewing, Clerk of Davidson County, Territory South of River Ohio. 2 May 1791.

p.132-133
To the Governor: John Ellis in answer to Mrs.Ann Gaillard's petition that she petitioned and obtained a grant in 1787 to the land in dispute. Ellis has a grant of older date. Mrs. Gaillard claims she has possession of sd land and has cultivated it for several years. It was with Ellis's permission, as Mr.Sanders and Mr.Vousdan declare.

p.133
Isaac Gaillard certifies he was person John Ellis lent land to, as his father was at Forse River and did not come up for 2 or 3 months. The Negro houses and crop was all on Ellis's land the first year. Isaac did not borrow that land; he knew it was vacant land.

Arbitrators chosen to settle dispute between Jeremiah Bryan and John Farguson determine Bryan to pay Farguson at rate of 100 Hard Dollars per year for time he was in his employ; the constable fees due Brian and Furguson and partnership profit to be equally divided. 2 October 1788. Justus King, Samuel Rainer, John Montgomery, Ezekiel [x] Duitt. Grand Pre

p.134
Opinion of G. W. Fitzgerald and J.Henderson, arbitrators betwixt Thomas Wilkins and Palser Shilling: Shilling to build kitchen chimney on the end next the dwelling house, to build house chimney on the end next the stable before cold weather sets in; he shall cover and board stable, and hang the door. Wilkins owes 15 Dollars per month from 15th April last until above work be completed and afterwards 20 Dollars per month. Natchez, 25 September 1788. Grand Pre.

Power/Attorney from Matthew Elliott and William Caldwell of Detroit to friend William Pauling of Detroit to recover money, debts, goods, payable and belonging to us. 14 Octr 1785, 25th year of His Majesty's reign. Witness: William Christie

p.135-136
Will of Richard Carpenter of the Natchez, merchant. To son James 800 acres lately granted by this Govt, situated 8 or 9 miles from the fort. A house 35 feet by 18 feet to be built thereon for my family. To wife Mary negro man Boston, negro woman Aimey, household furniture, white horse. To son James negro Kitty. To dau Mary Flowers negro Rose. To dau Elizabeth Bordeman negro Jack. Wearing apparel to be divided between wife, son, daughters and sons in law. House, lots at Natchez landing, 300 acres bought from John Luck to be sold. William Ferguson to dispose of property of Mr.Brown of Rhode Island. Residue equally divided between wife Mary, son James and 3 daughters Elizabeth, Mary, and Sarah. Executors: wife Mary, dau Mary Flowers, sons in law Daniel Flowers & Charles Boardeman, friends David Williams and Bernard Lintot. Property of two young children, James and Sarah, under care of Williams and Lintot. 4 cows and calves to wife Mary, 8 cows and calves equally to James and Sarah. 4 July 1788. Witness George Fitzgerald, George Proffet, Wm Vousdan, Peter Walker, Alex Henderson, Pierre Bissardon, J. Henderson

p.136
Mary Carpenter, Daniel Flowers, David Williams, Bernard Lintot, Alexander Moore to Lt.Col. Charles de Grand Pre: ask to be given estate books and papers and to be allowed to employ a person to draw up the books and debts.

p.136-137
Will of Ann Gaillard. To dau Ann Savage, negro fellow Badger now in her possession, feather bed, a wool and a moss mattress and a cherry bedstead. To niece Betsy Gaillard, negro man, boy, girl, 4 cows and calves. To dau Margaret Gaillard this plantation of three tracts total 700 acres, all stock, household furniture, horses, mules, ploughs. South Carolina land to be sold unless my children settle upon them. Divide money 1/4 to son Isaac Gaillard, 1/4 to dau Ann Savage, 1/4 to dau Margaret Gaillard, 1/4 equally to three grandchildren Benjamin, Anne Frances, and Peggy Farrar. Sixty Dollars/year for five years for education of two sons of Mrs. Phoebe Calvit. Twenty Dollars to Phoebe Calvit. Sixty Dollars/year for five years for education of two sons of John Lusk. Son Isaac Gaillard executor, daughters Ann Savage & Margaret Gaillard executrixes, they to be guardians of the three grandchildren named above. 3 November 1788. Wit: Sutton Banks, Margaret Taylor, Charles Surget, William Case, David Mitchell, Henry Roach. Carlos de Grand Pre.

p.138
New Orleans, 11 April 1789. Charles Norwood to Thos Wilkins. Enclosed letter from William Henderson promising to transfer to Norwood mortgage of 5 slaves Mr.Bankes made to him. Asks Wilkins to get him a copy of the mortgage.

New Orleans, 1 April 1789. Wm Henderson to Chas Norwood who holds a note jointly made by David Smith and Wm Henderson to James Frazer for 900 silver milled Mexican Dollars due since 18 August last. Wm being unable to make payment, as soon as he returns home to Natchez, Wm will transfer to Norwood, in behalf Frazer farther security for above sum-- Sutton Bankes mortgage for five slaves: Buckner, Kate, Eliza, Peter, and Bett, which mortgage shall be legally transferred before De Grand Pre; Wm consents to 10% interest on note until paid.

p.139
Bill of Sale, Andrew Goff of Washington County, Virginia, to Clark & Catherine Williams, Madison County, VA, negro wench about 25 years old named Larcy, mulatto child about eighteen month named Saley, price ninety pounds. 17 February 1789
Wit.: L.Williams, Jno Metcalfe, Wm Jones. Reg. 23 Dec. 1795

Bill/Sale Mary Palmer of Cecil Co, Maryland, to Adam Cloud,

Negro woman about 40 yrs old to serve 5 years from date; two children: Hannah about 4 to serve till she is 30, and Bet to serve till she is 30, which Cloud promises to free agreeable to above time. 7 October 1793. Witness: Wm Howell

Received of Lt.Col.Grand Pre, part payment of 4 negroes sold him by Daniel Park on acc[t] Henry O'Neill, Es[q], 500 Dollars. New Orleans, 29 March 1793. John Mayrother, Att[y] in Fact.

p.139-140
To Manuel Gayoso de Lemos. Jn[o] Girault, Manuel Gayoso de Lemos, Robert Shilling, Joseph Vidal, Estevan Minor. Deed from Polser Shilling, planter of Natchez, for 500 Dollars paid by Charles Watrous, physician, 125 acres bounded as expressed before. 13 June 1797.

p.140
Power of Attorney Samuel Bell to Richard Bell of Natchez, to collect a bond of Eight Hundred hard Dollars, in Natchez office, on Messrs Mordacai and Throckmorton. Natchez, 17 February 1791. Wit.: Charles McDonald, John [x] Green
Received of Samuel Bell in full of all accounts. 17 February 1791. Richard Bell. Wit: Charles MacDaniel, John [x] Green, Juan Girault.

p.140-141
Jeremiah Coleman and Elijah Swayzey, extrs, will of Gabriel Griffin decd, sell to Cato West, Es[q]., of Villa Gayoso Dis[t], Negroes Bob aged 40, Flora aged 30, Peggy aged 5 years, Hector aged 2 years, 800 Dollars paid. 19 Sep[t] 1797. Signed before John Foster and John Girault. Acknowledged by Jeremiah Coleman and Elijah Swayze, 19 September 1797. Juan Girault

p.141
Natchez, Second Creek Dist. Before Isaac Johnson, magistrate of Peace, afsd District, came Abram [x] Taylor who swears he sold corn to Charles Adams. Taylor asked payment; Adams said Caleb Biggs owed him money which he would get; Biggs paid a mare valued 40 Dollars. If Biggs paid 10 Dollars hard money Taylor would forget the rest. 10 October 1797. Juan Girault

p.142
4 Feb[y] 1797, bond of Samuel Wilson, Hawkins Co., TN, to John Foster, Natchez, to pay John Foster or his heirs $383.33 1/3 on or before 4 February 1799. Samuel (x) Lewis
Wit: Mordacai Hagood, Thomas Johnson. Juan Girault

Bill/Sale Richard Harrison planter of Natchez Dist, to Hardy Perry of Chicasau Nation, trader, Negro Cabboy, 450 Dollars of which 30 pd, 420 to be paid in horse cattle by 15 August next at Perry's plantation. Chicasaus, 8 Sep[r] 1791. Negro Cabboy warranted. Witnesses: Edward Richey, David Roberts. Before Gov.Don Manuel Gayoso Lemos, Captain Richard Harrison acknowledged full payment. Natchez, 2 June 1797

p.142-143
Bill of Sale, Garret Rapalje of Big Black, Natchez Dis[t], to Hardy Perry for 550 Dollars paid, Negro Sally age twelve. 1st February 1791. Witness: Jaques Rapalji. Juan Girault

p.143-144
9 November 1897(sic). Daniel Douglass, District of Natchez, West Florida, for 25 Dollars paid by heirs of Gabriel Griffin represented by his executors Cato West, Es[q], and Jeremiah Coleman, sells 200 acres situated about 30 leagues north of Fort Natchez on the south side of Big Black River, bounded by the river in front, east by Ezekial Newman's land, by Gabriel Griffin's land on the west, it being the same tract that was granted to Daniel Douglass for military services by patent, 10 January 1794. Signed in presence of John Corner and John Girault, before Stephen Minor, Governor Pro Tem of Natchez. Acknowledged 18 November 1797.

p.144-145
John Still Lee and Elizabeth Still Lee, Natchez, for $600 p[d] by John Girault, Natchez, sell Negro Bella age about 26 y[rs], American born, and her child, Rose, about 2½ years. Ack. before Stephen Minor, Gov.Pro Tem, 5 Dec 1797. John Still Lee. Elizabeth W. Still Lee. Witness: William Moss, Thomas Tyler. 6 Dec 1797. Ack.before Estevan Minor in presence of William Vousdan and Windsor Pipes

p.145
Bill/Sale, Charles Grigsby, Hawkins Co., to James McMullin, Negro Sally, age 13, for 72 lbs 10 shillings Virginia money, receipt ac[k] 8 December 1796. Wit.Melton Ford, Anthony Watson 25 August 1797. James McMullen signs over within B/S to John Foster for value received. Witness: Robert [R] Sheffield. Before Stephen Minor, Gov.pro tem, Jn[o] Foster, Natchez Dis[t]. ack.value rec[d]; made over within sale to Elias Bonel of this Dis[t]. 12 Feb[y] 1798. John Foster. Estevan Minor. Juan Girault

p.145-146
Certification that James Fletcher of New Orleans about four years ago employed me to find someone to settle his land between Fairchilds Cr & Coles Cr. I employed Samuel Chitester three years ago who has done his duty by clearing six acres, building a cabin upon it. He is now entitled to a deed from Fletcher for 200 acres of sd survey to be laid out on a long square adjoining any side, but not to include improvement he

made or any part of it nor deprive Fletcher of the water.
27th January 1798, Natchez. William Vousdan

p.146
Bill/Sale. Samuel Chitester of the Natchez, for $150 note of David Greenleaf, sell him above mentioned two hundred acres. 21 Feb 1798. Samuel Chitester. Wit. John Foster, William Gillespie. Ack. before Stephen Minor

p.146-147
Patrick Foley relinquishment to Mrs. Martha Davis of all his claim to her estate. November 9th 1790. Patrick Foley
Test: C. Percy, James Nicholson
Before Capt. Joseph Vidal, Gov.Pro Tem of the Natchez, James Nicholson of Houmachito Dist. proves his own signature above in presence of late Charles Percy saw Foley sign and acknowledge same. 19th March 1798. Joseph Vidal

p.147
Agreement, 14 Dec 1797, between John Ellis Senr and Anthony Hutchins both of the Natchez. Ellis sold Hutchins 320 acres granted to Richard Ellis Junr deceased, bounded on north by Nathaniel Tomlinson, south by Ellis's land, east by Dixon's tract now Ellis's land, west by Caleb Hutchins. Ellis agrees to make title to Anthony Hutchins on payment of $310, $50 to be paid on date, $50 on next Christmas, $210 in two or three months afterwards.
Wit. Samuel Tuel, William Mulholen.
Received from Anthony Hutchins $50, 14 December 1797 the sum first mentioned in within agreement. John Ellis Senr
Received from Anthony Hutchins Fifty Dollars, second payment mentioned, January 15th 1798. John Ellis Senr
Received from Anthony Hutchins corn to amt of Ten Dollars at same time. John Ellis Senior
Acknowledgment before Governor Pro Tem Don Joseph Vidal by Wm Mulholen that John Ellis and Anthony Hutchins Esq. signed within and above as their act and deed. 22 March 1798
Joseph Vidal. Registered 23rd March 1798. John Girault

p.148
Deed/Gift, Mary Higdon of Natchez Dist, Louisiana province, to grandsons Daniel Higdon and John Higdon of sd Dist, 2 Negro boys. To Daniel, Abram about 4 yrs old, & to John, Dick about 2 years old, both after my death. 16 March 1798. Mary (M) Higdon Wit. Russell Bean, E. Hoskins. Proven before Joseph Vidal, Gov.Pro Tem, by Russell Bean, Ezekiel Hoskins at request of Jeptha Higdon, 21st March 1798. John Girault

p.148-149
Deed. 28 February 1798, William Collins, Villa Gayoso Dist.,

Natchez, farmer, to Ebenezer Rees of St. Catherine District, Natchez, merchant. For 276 Dollars money of government afsd pd to Wm Collins, 500 acres in Feliciana District, Province of Louisiana, bound southwest by branch of Thompsons Cr, se and ne by vacant land, nw by William Dunbar. Wit. Edward Randolph, Charles F.Todd, John Nailer.
Written on back: Feb 28. Rec^{d} 276 Dollars in full for within mentioned tract. William Collins. Wit. Edward Randolph, Charles F. Todd, John Nailer
23 March 1798. Sutton Bankes, a magistrate for Natchez gov^{t} certifies witnesses ack^{d} deed. Foregoing deed registered at request of Ebenezer Rees, 24 March 1798. John Girault

p.149-150
7 March 1798. Lacy Rumsey, Villa Gayoso Dis^{t}, Natchez Gov^{t}, planter, to Ebenezer Rees, 400 Dollars paid, sells 500 acres in Pine Ridge Dist, Natchez, bound n by George Fitzgerald, w by Gabriel Benoist, s and e by Ebenezer Rees's land. Witness Charles F.Todd, Peter Walker, George Cochran.
Written on back: 7 March 1798 Recd of Ebenezer Rees 400 Dollars in full. Lacy Rumsey. Deed proved before Isaac Johnson, a Justice/Peace, Natchez District by George Cochran and Chas F. Todd proved deed. Recorded 24 March 1798 John Girault.

p.151
14 March 1798. John Still Lee & wife Elizabeth Still Lee of Bayou Pierre Dis^{t},Natchez Gov^{t}, to Ebenezer Rees of St.Catherine. For [blank] Dollars, 764 acres bounded e by Harkey, Carter, Perkins. n by Fulton, w by DeWit and Armstrong. Witness: Edward Randolph, Henry Milburn. Deed ac^{k} by John Still Lee, 16 March 1798. Edwd Randolph swears that Mrs.Elizabeth Still Lee acknowledged within to be her free act. Proved before Cato West, 16 March 1798.

p.152
Power of Attorney, Charles F.Todd formerly of Montgomery Co. Pennsylvania, now of St.Catherine Dist, Government of Natchez, appoints William A.Todd of Chester County, Pennsylvania, his attorney to recover his claims in Penna. 24 March 1798. Charles F. Todd. Proven before Joseph Vidal, Gov.Pro Tem. Recorded at request of Dr.C.F.Todd. 16 Mar 1798. Jno Girault

p.152-153
16 March 1798. Elizabeth Douglas of Villa Gayoso District, Natchez Govt, to Ebenezer Rees, St.Catherine Dist., 400 Dollars, 400 acres in Villa Gayoso Dist, bound sw by Cato West, other sides vacant. Elizabeth [x] Douglass now Elizabeth Leighliter. Witnesses: Edward Randolph, Nathaniel Brown. Recorded 26 March 1798 at request of Ebenezer Rees

p.153
Deed. Calvin Smith, planter, to David Mitchel, planter. Both of Natchez Dist. 400 acres, 400 Spanish milled dollars. Good title to be made. Calvin Smith. Acknowledged before Estevan Minor, recorded 26th March 1798. John Girault

p.153-154
Deed. 27th March 1798, John Ellis Senr to Col.Anthony Hutchins, both of Natchez District, for Three hundred ten Dollars paid, 320 acres in Houma Chitto District bounded by land of Miss Hutchins, Nathaniel Tomlinson, Richard Ellis & John Ellis, land granted to Richard Ellis Senr and by his executors conveyed to sd John Ellis Senr 22 Feb last.
Wit: William Neelly, John Girault. Acknowledged. J. Vidal
Registered 27th March 1798. John Girault

p.155
New Orleans, 25 April 1789. [Three illegible names] letter to Charles de Grand Pre. Anthony Hutchins having executed a mortgage before you in favor of 5 Negroes: Tim, Jaco, Sampson, Patte, Kitte, as security in lawsuit with Samuel Steer, and sd Hutchins long since termined sd suit and paid balance against him. Please give him a full acquittance and release his mortgaged negroes.

Thomas Wilkins of Mississippi Territory relinquishes claim to tract mentioned in mortgage, 846 acres. Natchez, 13 Novr 1798. Witness: Aaron Grugg, John Girault.

New Orleans, 22 April 1789. James Mather having settled with Matt White for the amount of his debt, asks acquittance before Commandant at Natchez to discharge the mortgage on his property as a security to Mather.

p.156
Will of John Perkins, Natchez District. One third of estate to wife Mary, one-third to child is pregnant with, one third to brother David Perkins. Friends Robert Miller and Charles Collins executors. 18 Jany 1789. Witness: Richard King, John Griffing, John Bell, Justus King, Prosper King, Aswell(?)[x] Yarbrough.

Natchez, 4 Nov 1789. Benjamin Farar to Isaac Gaillard, Executor, Mrs.Anne Savage & Margaret Gaillard, executrixes, will of Mrs. Ann Gaillard. Asks that when they go to New Orleans with their crop they will also take estate accounts, papers, books, their father's and mother's wills, and also a deed of gift by which they pretend to deprive his children of a part of what was given them by their grandmother. Sends letter by James Kelly and keeps a correct copy to prove that they have been given timely notice.

p.156-157
Benjamin Farar's petition to Governor Manuel Gayoso. Lachlan McNeil of Jamaica Island owes Farar 90 Dollars 7 Ryals. Enclosed statement of debt. Executors of Mr. Carpenter have a negro woman property of sd McNeil. Prays order to sell Negro and pay the debt. Natchez, 7 October 1789
1784 bill for medicines for McNiel's Negro wench... 90.7

p.158
Deed, John White, farmer, of Natchez, to Richard Harris and Caleb Owins of New Orleans, for 162 Dollars paid, 240 acres granted White by Gov.Mero on east branch Saint Catherine Cr, bounded by land of Daniel Waltman. 9 February 1785. Witness: --- Hutchinson, John Murray.

p.158-159
Will of Henry Stampley of Natchez Dist, planter. Son Jacob Stampley to care for youngest son William till age 21. Wife Margaret Stampley. To son Jacob Stampley plantation of 350 acres adj. Liddell Holt, cow & increase, all hogs except one sow. To son Peter Stampley 2 cows & increase, 1 small rifle. 10 October 1780. Witnesses Samuel Henry, David Holt.
Codicil: Jacob Stampley promises to take care of his father during his life in harmony. 10 October 1780. Witness Samuel Henry

p.159
Petition of Bettey and Jude to Gov.Miro. Daughters of a free woman in the Carolinas & apprenticed until they were age 21, they were brought to Natchez as such, but were took by Capt Willing's party and sold as slaves. Have served years beyond time of indentures. Pray governor to liberate them.
New Orleans, 21 March 1789.

Certification that Samuel Bell & Miss Rebecca Berry (Perry?) were married 28 May 1782 by Justus King according to Church of England form by consent of Rev.Mr. Savage.

p.160
Coles Creek, 11 July 1789. Jesse Hamilton, Wm Erwin, John Martin give opinion that Henry Jones shall pay eight Dollars or make 800 good fence rails on Mr. Perry's plantation or on such part as Mr. Perry shall choose.

Order from Grand Pre, 8 June 1789, to Wm Irwin, Jno Martin & Jesse Hamlinton to determine whether mulatto Henry Jones has worked twenty days as he claims, also if negroes Perry lent Jones have worked, and examine the difference between Perry and Jones respecting days worked and days claimed.

Statement by Philip P. Turpin. He cannot prove that Mr.Weeks broke into his-- Turpin's-- house and broke his gun; Turpin repeated what Elijah Swayze told him of Weeks's threatening to prevent Turpin from shooting. Natchez, 21 July 1789.

Natchez, 21 July 1789. Philip P.Turpin promissory note: will deliver to William Weeks next March for his stepson Stephen Sweezy a likely mare and colt, mare not over 8 years old, in consideration for Sweezy's mare that Turpin shot.

p.161
Bry(?) Bruin to Col.Charles De Grand Pre. Declines acting as arbitrator between Dr.Farar and Mr.Gaillard as DeGrand Pre's letter of the 11th asked, owing to his wife's alarming illness. Sends respects to Madame Grand Pre. [no date]

Natchez, 17 June 1790. Isaac Gaillard requests Gov.Grand Pre to allow him to consult with his sisters about nomination of an arbitrator, Col. Bruyn having declined to act in the dispute between Dr.Farar & estate of Tacitus Gaillard.

Natchez, 30 June 1790. Carlos de Grand Pre requests that the arbitrators between Benjamin Farar and Isaac Gaillard, executor of estate of Tacitus Gaillard and Mrs. Ann Gaillard, be immediately furnished with with authentic accounts of debts, crops made. Translation by J.Girault.

p.162
Isaac Gaillard, Anne Savage, Margaret Ellis, extrs estate of Tacitus and Ann Gaillard, declare the Negroes in division by arbitrators between Benjamin Farar and estate, are all that are part of the estate. A bond from Mrs.Elizabeth P.Cuny, of date South Carolina, 23 March 1777, for 2297 pounds SC money is all security in our possession for money due said estate.

Natchez, 30 June 1790. Alexander Moore and Sutton Bankes arbitrators between Benjamin Farar and extrs estate of Tacitus Gaillard: there is a balance of 3432 Dollars 7 rials and 1/4 due to Benjamin Farar, but arbitrators acted without satisfactory vouchers, and if any party should, within 18 months, produce farther documents, opinion to be reconsidered. Also, Deed of Gift 9 August 1763 is valid, and Dr.Benjamin Farar's children are entitled to their deceased mother's share. Also Miss Margaret Gaillard now Mrs.Margaret Ellis is entitled by her Father's will to the fifth part of the negroes only. Dr. Farar to be guardian of his children after giving security.

p.162-163

Natchez, 24 July 1790. Alexander Moore, Sutton Bankes, Bernard Lintot, Isaac Johnson made final division of the estate as far as Dr.Farar is concerned: 2967 Dollars 3/4 rial owed Benjamin Farar. His children are entitled to an equal fourth part of all debts. Have divided negroes in deed/gift. After taking out negroes left by wills of Tacitus Gaillard and Ann Gaillard to their daughter Margaret Gaillard and their niece Elizabeth Gaillard, made division of residue thereof agreeable to will of Ann Gaillard. Financial details stated.

p.163-164
Natchez, 31 August 1791. Isaac Alexander, Robert Ford, apptd by Gov. Gayoso to adjudge damage sustained by Robert Abrams by sale of his plantation, crop, stock, and working utensils to Samuel Martin late of Natchez Dist., but now of Chicasau Nation, say Abrams sustained damage of 158 Dollars 1 Ryal

p.164
Natchez, 26 Augt 1791. Inventory of buildings, stock, crop, utensils on plantation sold to Samuel Martin by Robt Abrams

Mississippi Territory, Adams County. Thomas Wilkins received full payment for mortgage. 8 April 1800. Wit: Peter Walker

Natchez, 25 April 1790. John O'Connor, Pierre Surget, G.W. Fitzgerald chosen by Grand Pre to decide between John Smith and William Falconer are of opinion that John Smith owes Mr. Falconer 102 Dollars 10 ryals.

p.165
New Orleans, 13 April 1790. Sutton Bankes states that 3 Novr 1788 he draw Last Will & Testament of Mrs.Ann Gaillard. She stated it might appear strange to bequeath part of estate to children of Dr.Benjamin Farar who is rich, but it was their right as children of her dau. Elizabeth Farar. who had never received anything. Wit: T.J.Duforest, Nicholas --

Natchez, 17 June 1791. Obediah Brown and Richard Corey, dispute decided by arbitration, consent to the award: Corey to deliver to Brown Corey's wife's stock and property & 45 Dollars. Brown to give Corey a feather bed and bedding, a gray mare and increase.

Benjamin Farar of Saxegotha Township, Berkley County, bound to Tacitus Gaillard, St.Matthew Parish, County afsd, 16,000 pounds money of Province to be paid to Tacitus Gaillard. 17 November 1774(sic); condition he pay 8000 pounds lawful money of province with interest thereon till paid, on or before 1 January 1766(sic). Wit: Moses Vance

p.166
White Cliffs, 4 July 1790. Ordered by Col. De Grand Pre, we immediately visited Greenbury Dorsey's flat called *The Washington*, made fast to shore by White Cliffs, foundered, containing 54 hogsheads tobacco afloat in her and a quantity of hemp. John Ellis, Thomas Burling

Natchez, 15 July 1790. Sutton Bankes opinion in the dispute of Morris Stackpole and Dr.Louis Four: sd Stackpole is still indebted to Four, the balance of the amount of six hogsheads tobacco at 75 Dollars each which he ought to pay by ensuing crop. States reasons for his opinion.

p.166-167
Natchez, 15 July 1790. David Williams opinion in the dispute between Dr.Ford and Mr. Stackpole. Ford has no further claim on the latter. States reasons for his opinion.

p.167
Natchez, 16 July 1790. Bernard Lintot's consideration of the opinions of Bankes and Williams in dispute Maurice Stackpole and Dr. Louis Four over six hogsheads of tobacco received by doctor from Mr.Stackpole. Agrees with Bankes that Stackpole ought to make good to Dr.Ford the sum for which he delivered the tobacco. States reasons for his opinion.

p.167-168
4 July 1790. Elijah Caneley, son of William Caneley decd, voluntarily apprenticed himself to his brother-in-law, John Clarke, wheelwright, to learn the trade during a term of 2½ years. Witness: William Clark, Richard Boddey. Gayoso.

Davidson County, North Carolina. 14 Feby 1789. Lardner Clark & Truman(?) Cartright swear they have frequently known hard money to be exchanged at the rate of 1 hard dollar for 5 paper in 1787 and 1788. Clark has exchanged at that rate. D. Hay, Justice of the Peace.
Davidson County, North Carolina, Andrew Ewing, Clerk of said County, certifies that David Hay is a justice of the peace

p.169
Natchez Dist, 15 Sept 1790. Ezekiel Forman to Charles Grand Pre. Grand Pre has not replied to his letter written on 10th requesting an inquiry. Since Mr.Chambers's stay is uncertain, he petitions: Natchez Dist, 15 Sept 1790. Ezekiel Forman to Hon.Chas Grand Pre. Young woman, Elizabeth Church, about 9th Aug last, died intestate at Forman's house. Petitioner heard reports of her property in this country. Wm Chambers is best source of information about her property, but Chambers daily

expects to leave this country.

In view of proposed marriage of Robert Miller and Miss Sarah Cole, inventory her property, 25 July 1790: 3 good mares, 2 good horses; 4 cows & calves; 3 3-yr old heifers, 1 4-yr old steer, 1 3-yr old steer, 5 hogs, 1 good bed and furniture; 1 good side saddle. Witnesses: John Searcy, Jacob Stampley, Solomon Cole. Rob[t] Miller's receipt for above, 25 July 1790

p.170
Will of Ann Bingaman, wife of Adam Bingaman, Natchez Dist, West Florida, planter. To Adam Bingaman, husband, also he to be executor. 7 March 1786. Witnesses: Patrick Foley, Samuel Gibson, Jacob Cobun

Will of Daniel [DP] Perry, Natchez District, West Florida, planter. All to wife Magdalane. Then, to eldest son Barnabas 326 acres on Second Creek, Negroes Hannah & Joe, boys Jack & Harry, cattle. Eldest daughter Rebecca Perry, Negro Chloe & expected child. Son Daniel 400 acres granted east of where testator resides, Negro Stephen. Dau Ann Perry, Boyd's Creek plantation on which I reside, Negro Dinah, 2 cows & calves. Daughter Lydia Perry Negroes Tom & Phillis, 2 cows & calves. If Rebecca offer Chloe for sale, wench shall become property of son Daniel. If dau Lydia survives, friend Isaac Johnson joint guardian with son Barnabas after death of wife Magdalane. Wit: Joe Funk Jr, Dennis Collins, John Martin, Stuart Higginson, Sebastian Derr, Isaac Johnson, Andrew Scondlin.

p.171-172
Will of Ralph Humphreys, Bayou Pierre, Natchez Dist, planter. Wife Agnes; sons George and Ralph; to Margaret McKenna a legacy of one hundred hard Dollars at age 16. Brother John Humphreys to be maintained. Wife and sons George and Ralph his executors. Witnesses: Mary Terney, Boyd and Bruin, John Burnet, Ezekial Johnson, Joseph Darlinton, Lewellin Price
Codicil. 29 March 1790. Considering wife's dowry, she is to have Negroes Cyrus, Sally & their children as her sole property. Witness: Matt Terney, Nicholas Grubb, Roderick ---, George Wilson Humphreys.

p.172-173
Deed: Thomas Green of Georgia, to sons Henry Green, Filmer Wells Green, Abraham Green, Everard Green: his Natchez property at Natchez, and his Negroes Charles, Tina, Bill, Selah, Dorcus, July, Florah, Benn, Friday, Nan, Arindes, America, Rachal, Fillis, Lero, Peter and Cuddy to be equally divided. 13 January 1785. Wit. N.Long, Wm Call

p.174

Will of Robert Davis, planter, of Georgia. Son Louis Davis, bed and slaves Bowlin and Phebe. Son Landon Davis, bed and slaves Sam and Sarah. Son Hugh Davis, bed and three slaves: Roger, Joe, Chockena. Wife Grace Davis, bed, negro girl Hannah, Negroes Charles, Peg, Harry & Jug. Son Nathaniel Davis 20 shillings. Son Isom Davis 20 shillings. Son Robert Davis 20 shillings. Daughter Abediah Floyo 20 shillings, daughter Sarah Burks 20 shillings, daughter Elizabeth Sexton 20 shillings (all money of Great Britain). Remainder to sons Lewis, Landon and Hugh, equally divided when Hugh comes to age 21. Executors sons Lewis Davis, Landon Davis. 5 September 1771. Witnesses: Thomas Shell, Mager Shell, Starling Shell.

p.175
Galvis Town, 12 June 1780. Certifies that Lewis, Landon, and Hugh Davis settled estate of Robert Davis dec[d]. Lewis Davis rec[d] Negro woman Cate in full for debt due him from estate; the other equal part is Negro boys Jack and Simon. Received: Lewis Davis. Witnesses: Landon Davis, Hugh Davis.

Rebecca Ambrose's certificate that Lewis Davis told her that girl Nelly now at Mr. Davis's was his child; his mother Mrs. Davis, stated the child was his. On her way from Georgia to this country Nelly's mother came to Rebecca, thinking Lewis Davis was there, to oblige him to maintain the child. 13 Feb 1791. Homochitto. Witness: Thomas Ambrose

Ruffin Swayze certifies that girl Nelly living at Landon and Hugh Davis's house has always been known as a bastard child of Lewis Davis. Mrs.Davis, their mother, took the girl when a child. Feby 15, 1791.

During Lewis Davis's life I never heard him say or even insinuate that Nelly was not his child. R. Gray

William Scott certifies that girl Nelly living at Landon and Hugh Davis's house has, from his first acquaintance with Mr. Davis's family in 1776, been known as Davis's bastard; never heard Lewis Davis or anyone say contrary. 25 January 1791.

p.176
Deposition of Benjamin Grubb who lived near Thomas Green Sr, now of Natchez, on Congree River, South Carolina. For three years before removing here, Green was arraigned for cladestinely taking hogs and sheep, in both cases Green paid cost. He behaved as an unjust troublesome man. Manuel Gayoso De Lemos. Natchez, 23 March 1791.

Deposition of John Donaldson, Villa Gayoso Dist, John Jarret informed deponent he had rented from Thomas Green Junr place upon Bluff for one year, to care for Green's livestock on sd plantation. In the house loft there was one rifle barrel and one shot gun barrel [translator says remainder is illegible]

Deposition of John Donaldson, Coles Creek District, when Jno Jarret took possession of Thomas Green's house near Bluffs, Villa Gayoso in 1791, there was left in the house two large ropes for use of Flats, property of Col. Thomas Green, among other articles in sd John Jarret's charge. 6 November 1793. Natchez. Certified by John O'Connor.

p.177
Natchez District, Coles Creek, 15 Feby 1791. David Odom declared that after last Christmas his largest hog came to his house shot with a bullet in the side of head, bleeding, does not know who did it. Declares he has lost hogs and does not know what became of them.

Natchez Dis^t, Coles Creek, 15 February 1791. Thomas Calvit declares he has lost some hogs, but does not know who killed them. Test: Chris Bolling

Natchez District, Coles Creek, 11 February 1791. John Richey of Coles Creek declares last January he was working at Capt. James Elliott's house. Elliott hunted hogs, sometimes marked with a crop & a slit in one ear and a swallow fork in other, Elliott and William Fairbanks killed their wild hogs in conjunction. He never knew Col. Green or family to shoot hogs. Witness: Christopher Bolling

p.177-178
Coles Creek, 10 February 1791. Declaration of William Barefield concerning the secret hunting and killing of cattle & hogs; he had often heard of James Elliott and William Farebanks hunting with dogs and gun in the woods for hogs. Last Saturday he was at Farebanks house, thinks Farebanks had in his smokehouse near a thousand weight of "boryed" bacon. At present he has seven hogs in his pen for fattening. One of the seven carried Mr. Elliott's mark, and one not marked. He helped Mr. Richey kill his hogs, and found a bowl of shot in one of them and cut it out.

p.178
Nashville, 2 May 1792. Hadon Wells, ext^r estate of Christopher Lightholder, rec^d from Joseph Calvit, Natchez, 800 hard Dollars for use of s^d estate, being payment of note given by Calvit to Lightholder, 8 Septr 1788, deposited with William Gilbert at the Natchez by Lightholder. This is full receipt of demands against Calvit on s^d note.
Davidson County. This day Haydon Wells came before us, David

Hay and Lardner Clark, Justices of the Peace for s^d County, and acknowledged above receipt.
Territory of the United States of America South of the River Ohio. Davidson County. Andrew Ewing, Clerk of Court, certifies that David Hay and Lardner Clark are two Justices/Peace for Davidson County. 2 May 1791.

P.178-179
By virtue of an Order from Interim Governor Charles De Grand Pre, Natchez Dis^t, to arbitrate Thomas Reed ag^t Maurice Curtere about a barge, Wm B.Smith & Wm Vousdan chose David Ferguson as umpire: barge is Thos Reed's property. Out of balance of 20 Dollars he still owes for s^d barge, he is to pay suit expenses & pay residue of s^d 20 Dollars to Maurice Curtero. Natchez, 13 January 1791.

p.179
Bernard Lintot, Anthony Hutchins, Isaac Johnson, Peter Walker, app^{td} with concurrence of Rev. Father William Swayze, to determine between Landon Davis & Anna Carter who charges him with seduction under promise of marriage. Anna averres her child is his; Landon denies, alleging no correspondence with Anna Carter for over eleven months before child's birth, but had lived criminally with her formerly. Anna being unable to produce legal proofs of promise of marriage, we decide:

Landon Davis to purchase a young Negro girl for Five Hundred paper Dollars, to be chosen by an indifferent party, to be settled on the child, Anna and her family not to sell or dispose of said slave, it remains sole property of child. Davis to maintain child until of age to go into the convent. Landon Davis to pay Anna Carter 100 paper Dollars compensation. New Orleans, March 1789.

p.179-180
Memorial of John Eldergill. Mr.O'Connor is soon to depart to New Orleans; he owes Mr.McKiernan of this government considerable money. For near two years there has been lawsuit between memorialist and Mr.O'Connor; Eldergill prays O'Connor not be given passport until he deposits a sum sufficient to discharge every demand that may arise in consequence of lawsuit, also that O'Connor appoint a person to act as Attorney for him in this affair during his absence. [no date]

Dr.John O'Connor is ordered in case of absenting himself, to give sufficient security for results of depending lawsuit, & to appoint attorney with power to represent him in said lawsuit. Manuel Gayoso de Lemos. [no date]

14 April 1793. Bond of John Wylie, Jno Roberts, Jno (x) Murphy; bound to James Willcox, New Orleans, 120 Spanish Milled

Dollars to be paid 15 June 1793; Condition that they deliver to John B. McCarty of New Orleans 300 saw logs per contract with James Willcox.

p.180-181
Contract: John Baptist McCarty Esq, and Benjamin Steel, John Roberts, John Wylie. For two or three years, 1000 mill logs are to be delivered to McCarty's mill at rate of one dollar apiece, two-thirds payment at delivery, one-third when mill has done season's work. Two-thirds logs at be 10½ feet long squaring 15"; one-third, 14 feet long, squaring 12". All to be free from sap, without any defects. McCarty to assist in stoping the rafts; to receive 500 to 600 logs in fall, remainder in rise of river in Spring.
29 July 1792. Further agreement about delivery of logs.
Witnesses: Daniel Clark Jr, William Wikoff Sr.

p.181-182
Thomas Irwine to Manuel Gayoso, Esq. Answering Mr. Truly's memo of 6th inst, he bought four Negroes of me at 12 months credit, giving John Lum his security, and mortgaging the Negroes until paid. Last year when I found that Mr.Lum was not able to pay his own debts and Truly having sold one or more of the mortgaged Negroes and sent them to Appalusous without my knowledge, I asked him for Counter Security. He gave sundry persons obligations for tobacco payable this year. These persons are not able to comply with their engagements as Jno and Richard Harrison is part of those securities to be paid in Kentucky tobacco to be brought down river this year by Mr Harrison who is not yet arrived. If others are ready to pay, please order them to deposit their tobacco where you direct. I can send security by Mr.McCarthy's boat next Saturday. Request not to exonerate Mr.Truly from his obligations for the payment of those Negroes through excuse of the papers being in New Orleans; papers can be here before debtors are ready to pay. Natchez, 9 February 1791

p.183
Deposition of Jacob Roads. Last October Roads was at plantation of John Adams when Maurice Stackpool asked him to settle his debt. After conversation, Stackpool told Adams that if he would give him notes he would approve of to the amount of Twenty Dollars, he would give him acquittance. After examining sd notes, Stackpool finding them unsatisfactory, the settlement did not take place. Adams asked Stackpool to give a receipt for money Arthur Cobb had been his security for. Stackpool would give no receipt as he did not approve of the notes. It appeared to deponent there was only 20 Dollars due by Adams to Stackpool; some mention of beaver hats. Manuel Gayoso de Lemos. Wit: John Girault, Stephen Minor. [n.d.]

Coles Creek, 12 Feb[y] 1791. George (X) Harris deposes he was at house of late Frederick Calvit when Arthur Cobb delivered Calvit's stud horse. Horse was hurt while in Cobb's possession. Calvit being sure horse would die, Cobb agreed to pay either whole price of horse or part, deponent unsure which. Horse did die. Witness: Cato West

p.183-184
Natchez, 20 October 1791. Agreement between Joseph Balinger of Kentucky now in this District and David Ferguson. Joseph Balinger sold in Apalousaws Country three Negro slaves and other property, part his own and part belonging to Ferguson, proceeds now in his possession in this District in cash and horses, which property they intend to dispose of in Kentucky for tobacco, they enter partnership for two years, Balinger & Ferguson. Witness, G. Cochrane.

p.184-185
Will of Frederic Calvet, Natchez Dist. Wife Mary one-third of property. My children Elizabeth, William, Lucretia, Mumford, Alexander, Joseph, remainder of property to be equally divided when they come of age. Bequest to Rachel Spikes poor orphan I brought up: mare, two cows and calves when she come of age. Wife extrx and John Bisland, Thomas Maston Green and brother Thomas Calvit executors. Natchez, 22 September 1790. Witness: John Short, Ebenezer Green, Gerard Brandon, Gabriel Griffing, William Daniel, Louis Alston.

p.185
Natchez District. Will of Ezekial (E.D.) DeWitt. All to wife Mary; at her decease, equally divide half to Catholic Church in Natchez, other half to Stephen Brashears. Negro girl Margaret to have full freedom as soon as she come of age. Executors Stephen Minor, Sutton Banks. 21 March 1791. Witnesses: John Short, Jas Elliott, Benjamin Grubbs, John Foster, John Potter, Thos Jordan

On 6 June 1789 Roger Dixon arrived in Natchez Dist from Virginia and brought with him 15 Negro slaves, 5 being property of Lucy Dixon his mother: viz three fellows Billy, Gloster and Peter, a blacksmith; 4 are property of Lucy Dixon Jr his sister: wench Fanny, girl Jenny, boys George and Lewis. Two are property of Robert Throckmorton his brother-in-law who hath taken them into his possession. Remaining four: Major a blacksmith, wench Patience, girl Rose, small boy Gloster are property of Roger Dixon. Dixon has power to sell on account of owners or to settle them on plantations as he finds more suitable. Dixon being about to journey to Virginia, leaving them on a plantation on Coles Creek, thinks proper to have foregoing account recorded in the governor's secretary's office. 14 May 1791. Roger Dixon.

p.186
John Girault, Keeper of the Records of this District, certifies that a mortgage was by agreement of parties, cancelled. Robt Miller gave up to attorney of Baptiste, land mortgaged for agreed sum, to be deducted from whole debt; after a settlement made between parties by John Eldergill, Miller gave his note for the balance. The attorney of Stayley agreed to receive of Hezekiah Williams from whom Miller had bought the land, his obligation for the titles thereof, and promised to meet Williams next morning to do the business. I attended & so did Hezekiah Williams, we remained, but none of the other parties appeared. Natchez, 16 May 1798.

20 March 1806 Job Routh personally appeared at Record Office of Spanish records of this Territory. Routh, lawful agent of John Baptist Staily, mortgagee in foregoing deed, ack[d] that mortgage is cancelled by mortgager's having paid Staily 200 Dollars and conveyed to him the af[sd] land. John Girault, Keeper of Records. J.P.Thomas (check initials.....)

p.186-187
William Dunbar's receipt to the administrator of the estate of Jacques Rapalje for payment of amount due upon a mortgage of Negro Joe, mortgaged by sd Jacqes Rapalje's father, said mortgage having been deposited in government archives during the administration of Governor Gayoso. 1 March 1804

p.187
Will of John Shannan, formerly of Ireland, now inhabitant of Natchez, Louisiana Province, Kingdom of Spain, carpenter and joiner. Estate to pay his debts; any over-plus to be divided among those who attended him in his last illness. Natchez.16 December 1791. Witness: Ebenezer Dayton, Solomon Swayze, Jn[o] Carroll, Valantine Thomas Dalton, Samuel Swayze, John Scott, Robert Patton, John Thomas, William Swayze

p.188
Natchez. 15 June 1792. Petition, W.Dortch to Governor. Some time ago he exchanged with George Overacre a Negro woman for a plantation and cattle. James Truly had sold sd plantation to Overacre. Dortch has been informed that the plantation he bought was property of Wm Ferguson; Overacre knew & deceived Dortch. Transaction unlawful, asks for return of property.

Natchez. 11 September 1792. Petition of Abner Marble to Gov. Manuel Gayoso de Lemos. Marble has an orphaned brother and sister, boy living with David Douglas, girl with his brother

in law John Arden. Children unable to endure the hard work. Marble asks that children chuse their own places. There are four more children besides these to be provided for.
Gayoso commands children, David Douglas, & John Arden to attend at Governor's House next Saturday.

p.189
Boat *Experiment,* property of John Rhea, Bardstown, Kentucky, loaded with tobacco and other things, was lost 22 June 1790 in Beach Fork River by striking an underwater rock. Tried to save her; current carried her off, nearly broken to pieces. When driven ashore, only two hogsheads tobacco left. Continued journey on Rhea's other boat, *Success.* 23 June 1793.
Boatmen: Henry (x) Stevens, Joseph (s) Lewis, Richard (x) Cowen. Check names.

Natchez, 9 April 1792. John Majrother, attorney in fact for Henry O'Neill, Esq., to Gov. Gayoso. Prays that Negroes now Mr.Jesse Greenfield's possession, property of Henry O'Neill, Esq, be returned, as the other planters did on demand, being satisfied the loss is to the owner. Mr. Rees, best security to Mr.Greenfield. Negroes to be returned and hire paid.

p.190
Natchez, 29 December 1792. The opinion of Bernard Lintot and William Dunbar as requested by the Governor, in the dispute between Messrs. Clark & Rees and Mr. Wilkins.

Natchez, 24 November 1792. Thomas Wilkins to Gov.Gayoso asking why Clark & Rees have not settled with him.
Natchez, 1 December 1792. Gayoso to Daniel Clark, Ebenezer Rees and Thomas Wilkins.

p.190-191
New Orleans, 25 April 1792. Maurice Stackpoole to John Joyce enclosing notes of Jacob Phillis for 142 Dollars, & notes of John Armsby for 162.6 Dollars. Phillis and Armsby have gone towards Mobile and Pensacola and will push for America. Mr. Phillis is about 5 ft 10 inches, fair with good complexion, dark hair, about 25 or 26 years old, rather slender. He has his own remarkable stout, able Negro with him, named Ben, 2 horses. Armsby is about same age, taller and stouter. Do not lose time seeking these people. Let me know your success.

p.191-193
Natchez. 7 November 1792. Petition of Maurice Stacpoole to Governor, explaining his business and financial arrangements with Jacob Phillis. Early this year Phillis went to Opelousas after Ormsby who Phillis said was indebted to him. Your petitioner put Phillis's notes in the hands of Mr.John Joyce

his attorney. Asks the governor for arbitration.

p.193
Natchez, 14 Decr 1792. F.W.Green certifies that about 1 to 4 June last he applied to Moses Bonner for 30 bushels corn and presented John Short's order for that quantity, Short showed him the corn referred to which was rotten. The corn crib was not covered to keep out rain.

p.193-194
Thomas Calvit, representative of Frederick Calvit, vs Arthur Cobb, respecting a horse. Referred to Ezekial Forman, Samuel Flowers and William Vousdan, 14 July 1792, a hearing on 27th postponed until 10 August, again until 14 Novr. John Bowls quotes Cobb at the landing, "Damn the horse, he is bad, and if he dies, I shall have him to pay for." Calvit told Robert Abrams he had got it from Cato Montgomery for a swift horse, put him in Cobb's hands to try if he was swift. Abrams asked Calvit how his horse was; was told he was dead. Abrams said, "that fool has killed him at last." Soon after horse died, Calvit told James Truly "his entrails were all decayed. John Smith & Groves Morris testified. Referees give opinion that Cobb was not guilty of horse's death. 18 Decr 1792

p.195
Natchez, 15 October 1792. Petition of Melling Wooley to governor. May 1789 Wooley bought slave from Mr. Wall, property of Francis Powset under mortgage to David Ross. Wooley being indebted to Moses Bonner for corn and land, sold him the Negro. Slave was taken by Mr. Vousdan, atty for Ross.
17 October 1792. Gayoso appoints Gabriel Benoist and Winston Pipes to estimate hire of above slave per month.
23 October 1792. Gabriel Benoist's estimate

Natchez, 3 October 1792. Petition of John Conner to Governor. Conner indebted to Mr. Swezey 7 Dollars. William Cock owed Conner 12 Dollars which he paid to Mrs. Swezey, but she would not give the overpayment to Conner.

p.197
Natchez, 3 October 1792. E. Minor orders Samuel Sweazey to pay John Conner without delay.

Papers of John Vousdan
10 October 1781. Note of Henry Manadue to Benjamin Kerkindal to pay a likely Negro between age 16 and 20 on or before 10 April next. Wit: Jacob Brown, Absalum Chrisom
On back: assignment by Benjamin Kerkendal to John Foster, 17 February 1786.

17 Feby 1786. Benjamin Kuykendall to Henry Manadue. Asks him to pay John Foster a likely young Negro for which Kuykendall had paid him in Carolina. Foster has paid. Kuykendall & Capt Prince will be there this Fall.

13 Feby 1786. Before Magistrate James Moldon, Absalum Chrissom swears Henry Manadue gave note to Benjamin Kuykendall.

p.197-198
19 October 1791. Note of Turner Williams. To pay John Foster a Virginia-born Negro woman age 14 to 20, to be delivered at Foster's house in Natchez District before next February. Wit: James Rhodes, Samuel (s) Jones.

p.198
Received 17 May 1792 of John Foster 200 Dollars in trade for property on Holsteen's River that he empowers me to recover. John (x) Honecut. Wit: Randall Gibson, John Ferguson.

Foregoing copies of papers are left in government office by John Foster. He carries originals to Cumberland. Natchez, 27 August 1792. Gayoso.

Natchez, 18 August 1792. Having been paid in full, Joseph Calvit presents document proved at Nashville and asks Excellency to order William Gilbert to give up Said note.

Natchez, 21 August 1792. Gayoso having heard William Gilbert and viewed copy of Christopher Lightholder's will, it is determined Mr. Gilbert shall give up note upon receiving a receipt from Mr.Calvit to annul receipt given by sd Gilbert to Christopher Lightholder. Gayoso. Natchez, 21 August 1792

p.198-199
Natchez, 18 August 1792. Joseph Calvit explains to Governor that in 1788 he gave his note to Christopher Lightholder for 800 Dollars, as security for John Montgomery. The note was deposited with William Gilbert (page missing)

p.199
Natchez, 18 August 1792. William Gilbert will return to Joseph Calvit the note mentioned in his petition. Gayoso

Natchez, 25 June 1792. Nathaniel Ivy to Governor. Mr.Wicks's negro shot petitioner's mare, one of only two he has to tend his crop with. Was told mare had jumped into Wicks's enclosure, but she did no damage, and they killed her before they notified him. Wicks (Weeks) will not pay animal's value.

Natchez, 26 June 1792. Ezekial Forman apptd to hear William

Wickes defence, order evidence, and give decision. Gayoso.

p.199-200
Natchez, 9 July 1792. Ezekial Forman, having heard the parties, decides William Wicks must deliver to Nathaniel Ivy an old gray mare, and one small bay mare with sucking colt.

p.200
Nathaniel (X) Ivey acknowledges receiving from William Wicks the mares as expressed in the award of Ezekial Forman.

Natchez, 15 May 1792. Petition of Morris Custard to Don Manuel Gayoso de Lemos. Had 190 bushels of corn put into a crib on Isaac Gaillard's plantation where the corn grew; this was petitioner's share. Owed 50 bushels of it to Isaac Gaillard. Custard sold remainder to William Dunbar, but cannot deliver because Gaillard has taken all Custard's corn from the crib.

Gayoso decided that Isaac Gaillard was authorized by DeGrand Pre, comdt in Gayoso's absence, to remove the corn lawfully owed him by Custard. Remainder was not put into his care and Custard broke into the crib without his knowledge. Arbitration costs to be paid by Custard.

p.200-201
Natchez, 28 April 1792. Arbitrators' opinion: Isaac Gaillard to give Job Corry's note for 17 Dollars and his own certificate to Maurice Custard and Henry Willis' note for 5 Dollars 2 rials. Custard is immediately to repair Gaillard's blacksmith tools in Custard's possession, reparation to be judged by Jno Lusk, to deliver to Gaillard 60½ bushels corn, pay 13 Dollars for accounts presented to sd arbitrators. Wm Dunbar, Jno Girault

p.201
Natchez, 9 April 1792. William B. Smith, umpire between John Smith and Gibson Clark, arbitrators having disagreed. Smith alleges he suffered from Clark's abuse the loss of an eye & other injury. Clark to pay Smith 200 Dollars in grain, hogs, cattle, or horses at option of Smith, provided Smith makes a deposition to His Excellency that, being deprived of the use of an eye, he cannot earn his living by his trade. Witness: David Ferguson.

p.201-202
Agreement of Samuel Levi Wells to Mary Bonner, acknowledging his natural son. Wells is to give Mary Bonner 25 Dollars per annum for 10 years begining 1 December last, 1 complete suit of clothes, after ten years Wells may take his son under his care. Should Mary marry, Wells can claim his son. Security:

William Foster. Natchez, 21 March 1792. Mary's father Moses (M) Bonner accepts agreement. Certified by Don Manuel Gayoso de Lemos. Witnesses: Anthony Soler, Augustin Mccarty.

P.202-203
William Henderson secures his estate to his creditors during a planned business trip to the United States. Being Indebted to John O'Connor 5010 Dollars, he leaves with him titles to properties: 250 arpents on Big Black River granted to Squire Boon 18 October 1788 by Stephen Miro. Another, same. Another for 200 arpents in same place. Another for 100 arpents same place. One for 500 arpents granted Henderson on Homochitto. Also the plantation where Henderson resides, 3 Negroes mortgaged to Peter Saure. One Negro, 35 horned cattle, 6 horses, 5 horned cattle on plantation at Homochitto in hands of Mordecai Richards, one horse, 100 hogs. Ratified by Don Charles de Grand Pre. Witnesses: Jos Vidal, Valentin Rincorn

20 March 1810. Certification by J.Girault, Keeper of Spanish Records, that foregoing is faithful translation of original.

Will of David Munro, Natchez District. To nephew George Munro, Bremore Parish, County Caithness, North Britain, 2 Negro men George & Anthony, wench Hannah, and all other property. Executors David Ross, John Bisland, George Fitzgerald. July 20, 1791. Witnesses: Alex Grant, Jn° Short, William Barland, Thomas Freeman, Jacob Lightholder, William Hamilton.

p.203-204
Natchez, 7 May 1793. Decision of Manuel Gayoso De Lemos on a controversy among heirs of Sarah Truly: James & Benet Truly, Eleanor Spain, Martha Harrison. Estate to be divided as ordered by Sarah's will 15 March 1792 except 2 cows and calves to Eleanor Spain, remainder of cattle to Martha Harrison. James Truly, Benet Truly, Francis Spain, James Harrison.

p.204-205
Will of Sarah Truly, Natchez Dist. Her late husband Hector Truly made will in Virginia, leaving each child a Negro. As Extrx, she delivered Negroes except to youngest child Bennet Truly, who had no Negro or anything in lieu therefor. Therefore Bennet gets wench Annico with her small children, Sarah and Lucy. Bequests to sons James Truly, Bennet Truly, daughters Martha Harrison, Eleanor Spain after Debdel Holt breaks up housekeeping, to granddaughter Sarah Spain. All remaining estate to three children James Truly, Bennet Truly, Eleanor Spain. Executors Parker Carradine, James Truly, Bennet Truly and Francis Spain. 15 March 1792. Witnesses: Ezekial Forman, John Lum, William O'Connor, Eben Potter, William Hamilton.

p.205
Deed from Charles (X) Howard of Natchez District to James Brown, for 100 Dollars, plantation of Fairchilds Creek near John Stowers Plantation, it being the plantation where I now live and near lands of sd Brown, and all my right to vacant land adjoining thereunto. 15 February 1786 Witness: H. Manadue, Thomas (X) Griffin

INDEX TO NAMES AND PLACES

--, ANTHONY 40
--, BETSY 1
--, NELLY 57
--, NICHOLAS 54
--, RODERICK 56
ABRAM (slave) 49
ABRAMS 54 64
ADAMS 5 10 47 60
ADAMS COUNTY 31 54
AIMEY (slave) 45
ALBERTS 29
ALBERTSON 30
ALEXANDER 7 54
ALSTON 61
AMBROSE 57
AMERICA (slave) 56
ANNICO (slave) 67
ANTHONY (slave) 67
APALOUSAWS, APPALUSOUS 60 61
ARDEN 63
ARINDES (slave) 56
ARMSBY 63
ARMSTREET 16 30
ARMSTRONG 17 50
ATTAKAPAWS 38
BACON 1 3 6 8 10+ 13-16 30 42
BADGER (slave) 46
BAILEY 41
BAILLIE 39
BAKER (slave) 30
BAKER 10
BALINGER 61
BALK 18
BALL 20
BANKES 37 46+ 50 53 54+ 55
BANKS 32 41 46 61
BAPTISTE 62
BARBOUR & HARRISON 2 3 4
BARDSTOWN 63
BAREFIELD 58
BARLAND 21 67
BARNETT 10
BATON ROUGE 7 33
BAY & MACULLAGH 2
BAYOU PIERRE 30 31 50 56
BAYOU SARA, SARAH 21-24 26-30
BEACH FORK RIVER 63
BEALE, BEALLE 16 30
BEAN 49
BEATTY 20 21
BELK 16 18 30
BELL 32 43 47 51 52
BELLA (slave) 48
BEN, BENN (slave) 17 56 63
BENOIST 50 64
BERKLEY COUNTY 54
BERNARD 16 30
BERRY 52
BET, BETT (slave) 46 47
BETTEY, BETTY (slave) 18 52
BIG BLACK BAYOU/RIVER 30 48+ 67
BIGGS 47
BILLOO 7
BILLY (slave) 61
BINGAMAN 16 17 38 56
BINGAMON 3
BINGHAM, BINGHAMAN 3 16
BISLAND 7 16 19 38 42 61 67
BISSARDON 45
BLACKBURN 27 28
BLOMMART 2 3 6 13 15 17 18 19
BOARDEMAN, BOARDMAN 16 30 45
BOB (slave) 47
BODDEY 55
BOLLING 58
BOLLS 37
BONEL 48

BONNER 16 30 42 43 64+ 66 67
BOOKER 31
BOON 67
BORDEMAN 45
BOSLEY 1
BOSTON (slave) 45
BOWLIN (slave) 57
BOWLS 64
BOYD 2 56
BOYD & CARADINE 2
BOYDS CREEK 36 56
BRABARON 12
BRABAZON 13
BRANDON 61
BRASHEARS 61
BREMORE PARISH 67
BRESHARES 10
BRIAN 7 45
BRIANT 41
BRITAIN 67
BROCAS 30
BROCHUS 12
BROCURS 10
BROWN 31 33 45 50 54 64 68
BRUIN, BRUYN 30 53 56
BRYAN 12 45
BUCKNER (slave) 46
BUFFALO DISTRICT 22 23 30
BURK COUNTY 17
BURKS 57
BURLING 55
BURNET, BURNETT 16 17 20 56
CABBOY (slave) 47 48
CAITHNESS COUNTY 67
CALDWELL 45
CALL 56
CALVET 16 44 61
CALVIT 10 30 35 44 46 58+ 61+ 64 65
CANE (slave) 32
CANELEY 55
CARADINE 3
CARMACK, CARMICK 42 44
CAROLINA (state) 18
CARONDELET 38
CARPENTER 41 45 46 52
CARRADINE 2 15 18 67
CARROLL 62
CARSEY (slave) 1
CARTER 19 30 32 50 59
CARTIN 16
CARTRIGHT 55
CASE 4 9 46
CASTLES 16
CECIL COUNTY 46
CATE (slave) 57
CEZAR (slave) 32
CHACHERE 36
CHAMBERS 20 21 55
CHARLES (slave) 32 56 57
CHEROKEE INDIANS 37
CHESTER COUNTY 50
CHICASAU, CHICKASAU, CHICKASAUW, CHICKASAW NATION 7 8 39 40 47 48 54
CHITESTER 48 49
CHLOE (slave) 56
CHOATE 4
CHOCKENA (slave) 57
CHOCTAW NATION 40 41
CHRISOM, CHRISSOM 64 65
CHRISTIE 45
CHURCH 55
CLARK, CLARKE 12+ 13 15 20-23 44 55+ 59 60 63 66
CLARKSVILLE 21 22 23
CLEMANS 16
CLOUD 46 47
COALMAN 41
COBB 10 60 61 64
COBUN 14 38 56
COCHRAN, COCHRANE 50 61
COCK 42 64
COLE 12 20 56
COLEMAN 6 16 30 37 47 48
COLES CREEK 3 7 12 18 31 35 36 37 48 52 58 61+
COLLING 31
COLLINS 43 49 50 51 56
CONGREE RIVER 57
CONTOY 32
CONWAY 31
COOK, COOKE 43 44
COOPER 26 42
COREY 54
CORNER 48

CORNES 42
CORRY, CORY 8 66
COUGHLIN 35
COWEN 63
COXON 41
CRANE 1 8 9 11 12 40
CRAVEN COUNTY, SC 32
CREEK INDIANS 37
CUDDY (slave) 56
CUFFEY (slave) 17
CUMBERLAND 65
CUNY 53
CURTERE, CURTERO 59
CURTIS 16 30
CUSTARD 66
CYRUS (slave) 56
DALTON 62
DANIEL (slave) 32
DANIEL 61
DARLINTON 56
DARTT 16
DAVENPORT 37
DAVIDSON COUNTY 1 43 44 55 58 59
DAVIS 49 57 59
DAWES 17
DAY 12
DAYTON 62
DE GRAND PRE. See GRAND PRE
DELAVILLEBEAUVE 15
DENHAM 21-29
DENNON 44
DERR 56
DES HUBLES 31
DESSELINE 32
DETROIT 45
DEVAL, DEVALL 9 36 41
DEWIT, DEWITT 10 17 50 61
DICK (slave) 19 32 42 49
DINAH (slave) 56
DIXON 49 61 62
DOL (slave) 17
DONALDSON 57 58
DOTTEY (slave) 32
DORCUS (slave) 56
DORSEY 55
DORTCH 62
DOUGLAS 7 34 35 50 62 63
DOUGLASS 48
DRAKE 43 44
DUET, DUETT 17 41
DUFOREST 54
DUITT 45
DUKES 39
DUNBAR 31 37 50 62 63 66+
DUNCAN 36
DUNHAM 21
DURNFORD 9
DUVAL 35
EDWARD, EDWARDS 34 40
ELDERGILL 12 32 59 62
ELIZA (slave) 46
ELLIOT, ELLIOTT 11 12 31-37 45
ELLIS 6 11 13 14 15 16 30 32 44 45 49 51 53 55
ELSEY (slave) 32
ERWIN 52
ESPENEL (slave) 32
ESTHER (slave) 32
EUDGO (slave) 17
EWING 1 43 44 55 59
FAIRBANKS 58
FAIRCHILD CREEK 31 48 68
FALCONER 54
FANNY (slave) 61
FARAR 32 33 34 35 51 52 53 54
FAREBANKS 58
FARGUSON 10 45
FARLIE 2
FARQUHAR, FARQUHER 3 14 19 37 44
FARR 18
FARRAR 46
FARRELL 5 13
FARWELL 7
FEBE (slave) 17
FELICIANA DISTRICT 50
FERGURSONE 1
FERGUSON 2 3 4 5 8 11+ 15 20 41 45 59 61 62 65 66
FILIS, FILLIS (slave) 17+ 56
FINLEY 10
FITZGERALD 1 4 19 20 42 45+ 50 54 67
FITZPATRICK 17
FLETCHER 48 49

FLORA, FLORAH (slave) 47 56
FLORRY 32
FLOWERS 38 45 46 64
FLOYO 57
FOLEY 4 8 13 49 56
FOLSOM 39 40 41
FORD 16 30 48 54 55
FORMAN 20 21 30 55 64 65 66 67
FORNEY 8
FORRESTER 41
FORSE RIVER 45
FORT NATCHEZ 48
FORT PANMURE 2 3 31 38
FORT PITT 41
FORTUNE (slave) 32
FOSTER 7 16 30 42 47+ 48 49 61 64 65+ 67
FOULSOM, FOULSON 40
FOUR 55
FRANK (slave) 32+
FRASER, FRAZER 41 46
FREEMAN 67
FRIDAY (slave) 56
FUGERSON 10
FULSOM 12
FULTON 50
FURGUSON 45
FURNEY 7 8 9
GAILLARD 16 30 32 44 45 46 51 53 54+ 66
GALVEZ 33
GALVIS TOWN 57
GASPIT 18
GAYOSO DE LEMOS 16 20-22 30 47 48 52 54 55 57 59 60 62-67
GENDRON 32
GENEY 4
GEOGHEGAN 36
GEORGE (slave) 32 61 67
GEORGIA 56 57
GIBSON 9 11 16 38 56 65
GILBERT 18 32 58 65
GILLESPIE 49
GILLWRAY 3
GIRAULT 16 20 30 38 42 47+ 48 49 50 51 53 60 62 66 67
GLOSTER (slave) 61
GOFF 46
GOODWIN 20 29
GORDON 1
GRAFTON 16 30 37 42
GRAND PRE 1-11 13-15 18 31 34 37 41 42 44-47 51-55+ 59 66 67
GRANT 67
GRAY 30 57
GRAYDON 7 8
GREEN 12 15 33-37 40 41 47 56 57 58 61 64
GREENFIELD 63
GREENLEAF 49
GREGGS 43
GRIFFIN, GRIFFING 47 48 51 61 68
GRIGSBY 48
GRUBB, GRUFFS 56 57 61
GRUGG 51
GUNTER 21
HAGOOD 47
HAMILTON, HAMLINTON 32 39 52+ 67+
HAMPTON 43 44
HANKINS 10
HANNAH (slave) 29 47 56 57 67
HANSBROUGH 4
HARKEY 50
HARMON 10 15
HARRIETTE (slave) 32
HARRIS 52 61
HARRISON 3 4 7 9 18 47 48 60 67
HARRY (slave) 56 57
HATTEY (slave) 32
HAWKINS 5 10 17 18 29 30 40
HAWKINS COUNTY 47 48
HAY 55 59
HAYWOOD 33
HAZAR (slave) 32
HEADY 16 30
HEATHLEY, HEATHLY 7 10
HECTOR (slave) 47
HENDERSON 16 30 31 45+ 46 67
HENRY 6 52
HESTER (slave) 32
HIGDON 10 19 37 49
HIGGINSON 56
HILL 1
HILTON 29
HIORN 19

HISER 5 6
HOGGET 1
HOLLOWAY 7 33
HOLMES, HOLMS 9 12 13 16 30
HOLSTEEN'S RIVER 65
HOLSTON 37 42
HOLT 7 39 40 52 67
HOMES 11 15
HOMOCHITTO 30 31 57 67
HONECUT 65
HONLER 39
HOOPER 43
HOOPOCK, HOOPPOCK 4
HOOTOR 9
HOPPER 8
HORTON 21-29
HOSKINS 49
HOUMACHITO, HOUMA CHITTO DISTRICT 49 51
HOWARD 38 68
HOWELL 47
HUBBARD 13 15
HUMPHREYS 56
HUNTER 21+ 22 23+ 24 26 28 29 30
HUTCHINS 1 2 3 5 6 16 30 37 38 49 51 59
HUTCHINSON 52
HUTTON 26
INDIAN NATIONS 7 8 40 47
INDIANS 1 27 28 37 39
IRELAND 62
IRWIN, IRWINE 52 60
IVEY, IVY 16 30 65 66
JACK (slave) 45 56 57
JACKSON 31
JACO (slave) 51
JACOBS CREEK 41
JAMAICA ISLAND 52
JAMES (slave) 17
JAMES 40
JAMISON 40
JARRET 57 58
JELLIASON, JELLISON 2 3
JEMMY (slave) 32
JENNY (slave) 61
JETT 32 33
JINNY (slave) 17
JOAN (slave) 32
JOE (slave) 56 57 62
JOHNNY (slave) 32
JOHNSON 1 4 6 7 8 9 12 14 15 16 18 19 30 47+ 50 54 56+ 59
JOHNSTON 3
JONES 16 39 40+ 46 52+ 53 65
JORDAN, JORDEN 12 13 16 30 37 41 42 61
JOYCE 63+
JUBA (slave) 32
JUCS (slave) 32
JUDE (slave) 18 52
JUG (slave) 57
JULY (slave) 56
JUNE (slave) 17
JUPITER (slave) 17
KATE (slave) 33 46
KEES 31
KELLY 11 41 51
KENNEDY 4
KENTUCKY (state) 20 37 60 61 63
KERKENDAL, KERKINDAL 64
KIMBALL 22 24 27 28
KING 2 6 9 11 16+ 30 36 37 41 45 51 52
KING OF FRANCE 39
KIRK 42
KITTE, KITTY (slave) 45 51
KNOTTS 3
KUYKENDALL 65
LAMMENTON (slave) 17
LARCY (slave) 46
LEA 33
LE DUC 38
LEE. See STILL LEE
LE GRAND 32
LEIGHLITER 50
LEMONS 9
LEONARD 9
LERO (slave) 56
LEWIS (slave) 61
LEWIS 20 47 63
LIESTARD 42
LIGHTHOLDER 43 44+ 58 65 67
LIMBRICK (slave) 19
LINTOT 16 45 46 54 55 59 63
LINTOTT 30
LONDON, ENGLAND 2

LONG 56
LOPEZ 20 26
LOPEZ ARMENTO 38
LOVELACE 17
LUCK 45
LUCY (slave) 67
LUM 14 16 30 60 67
LUSK 9 66
MACARTY 16
MACDANIEL 47
MADDEN 37 38
MADISON 6
MADISON COUNTY 46
MAGGET 15
MAJOR (slave) 61
MAJROTHER 63
MANADUE 64 65 68
MANDAY (slave) 17
MANSHACK 13
MARBLE 62 63
MARGARET (slave) 61
MARMADUE, MARMADUKE 20 29 31 41
MARNEY 9 21
MARTIN 36 52 54 56
MARY (slave) 17
MARYLAND 46
MATHER 41 51
MAYES 11
MAYRANT 32
MAYROTHER 47
MAYS 11
McCABE 20
McCARTHY, McCARTY 60 67
McCONNELL 29
McDONALD 47
McGILLRAY 13
McINTOSH 1-4 8 11 13-16 38
McKENNA 38 56
McKEY 41
McKIERNAN 59
McMULLIN 48
McNEIL, McNIEL 52
McPHERSON 6
MELLING 38
MERO. See MIRO
METCALFE 46
MILBURN 50
MILLER 2 3 5 51 56 62
MINOR 12 16 17 19 30 32 33 35 47 48 49 51 60 61 64
MIRO 19 20 31 33 34 38 44 52 67
MISKLER 20
MISSISSIPPI TERRITORY 51 54
MITCHEL, MITCHELL 46 51
MOLDON 65
MOLLOY 43
MONSANTO 42
MONTGOMERY 18 44 45 64 65
MONTGOMERY COUNTY 50
MOORE 16 17 20 38 44 46 53 54
MORANDE 3
MORDACAI & THROCKMORTON 47
MORE 11
MORGAN 16 30
MORRIS 8 64
MORRISON 10
MOSS 48
MULHOLEN 49
MUNRO 67
MURDOCK 12 40 41
MURPHY 59
MURRAY 30 52
NAILER 50
NAN (slave) 56
NASHVILLE 44 58 65
NEELLY 51
NEW ORLEANS 3 8 10 11 14-20 31 32 38 41 42 44 46-48 51 52 54 59 60 63
NEWBERRY 39 40
NEWMAN 48
NEWTON 10
NICHOLSON 30 49
NORTH CAROLINA 17 43 55
NORWOOD 3 46
NOWLAND, NOWLIN 34 36
NUBEARY 39
O'CONNOR 54 58 59 67+
ODOM 9 58
OGDEN 22 23
OGILSBY, OGLESBY 16 30
OLD TOM (slave) 19
O'NEILL 47 63
OPELOUSAS, OPPALUSAW 20 63

ORAN 7
ORMSBY 63
OVERACRE 62
OWINS 52
PALMER 32 46
PARK 47
PARKER 24 25 26 27 28
PATIENCE (slave) 61
PATTE (slave) 51
PATTON 62
PAUL 18
PAULING 45
PEARY 32+
PEG (slave) 57
PEGGY (slave) 47
PENNSYLVANIA 20 50
PENSACOLA 2 5 9 33 63
PERCY 30 49
PERKINS 50 51
PERRY 9 47 48+ 52+ 56
PETER (slave) 39 40 41 46 56 61
PETERKIN 4
PHEBE (slave) 57
PHILLIS (slave) 56
PHILLIS 63
PINE RIDGE DISTRICT 50
PIPES 16 30 48 64
POINT COUPE 4 13
POLLOCK 18
POTTER 61 67
POUNTNEY 6 7
POWSET 64
PRESLER 30
PRESTLEY 16
PRICE 6 56
PRINCE (slave) 32
PRINCE 65
PROFFET 45
QUINAS 11
RABY 17
RACHAL (slave) 56
RAINER 45
RANDOLPH 31 50
RAPALIE, RAPALJE, RAPALJI 6 11 15 17 18 30 48 62
RAUPETO 30
RAYNER 44
REBEKAH (slave) 33
REED 16 59
REES 50+ 63
RENDALL 35
RHEA 63
RHODE ISLAND 45
RHODES 65
RICHARDS 67
RICHARDSON 36
RICHEY 48 58
RICKNOR 23 24 25 26+ 27 29
RINCORN 67
ROACH 26 46
ROADS 60
ROBERTS 20 47 59 60
ROBERTSON 6 11 18 43
ROGER (slave) 57
ROLLINGS 10
ROMEO (slave) 5
ROSE (slave) 37 45 48 61
ROSS 5 64 67
ROUTH 62
ROW, ROWE 4 5 10 14 24-27 29
RUMSEY 50
ST. CATHERINE CREEK 4 52
ST. CATHERINE DISTRICT 50+
ST. GERMAIN 20 29 30
SALEY, SALLY (slave) 46 48+ 56
SAM (slave) 57
SAMBO (slave) 17
SAMPSON (slave) 51
SANDERS 44
SANDY CREEK DISTRICT 26
SANTEE RIVER 32
SARAH (slave) 57 67
SARTORS 40
SAURE 67
SAVAGE 32 46 51 52 53
SCAGE 41
SCANLIN, SCANTLING, SCONDLIN 16 30 56
SCOTT 57 62
SCRUGGS 10
SEARCY 56
SECOND CREEK 5 14 20 47 56
SELAH (slave) 56
SERMAN 32

SEXTON 57
SHANNAN 62
SHEFFIELD 48
SHELBY 42
SHELL 7 57
SHILLIN, SHILLING 8 10 16 30 45 47
SHORT 8 10 21 29 42+ 61+ 64 67
SHUNK 11
SIMMONS 42 43
SIMON (slave) 57
SMALL 10
SMITH 1 3 4 12 15 17+ 18 19 22 23 27-31 34-37 41+ 42 46 51 54 59 64 66
SOLER 67
SONORA 33
SOUTH CAROLINA 46 53 57
SPAIN 9 67
SPELL 8 11 18
SPIKES 61
SPRIGGS 12
STACKPOLE 55
STACKPOLE, STACKPOOL, STACKPOOLE, STACPOOLE 55 60 63
STAILY 62
STAMPLEY 7 40 52 56
STANFIELD 6
STANLEY 12
STAYLEY 62
STEEL 60
STEER 51
STEPHEN (slave) 17 56
STEPHENSON 20
STEVENS 63
STILLEE 17
STILLES 42
STILL LEE 17 48 50
STILLY 33
STOWERS 43 68
STROTHERS 44
SUMNER COUNTY 43
SUMTER 17
SURGET 46 54
SUSIE, SUSY (slave) 32
SUTTON 43 44
SWANSON MCGILLVRAY & CO 41
SWAYZEY, SWAZEY, SWAYZE, SWEAZEY, SWEAZY, SWEEZY, SWEZEY 5 11 16 30 47 53 57 59 62 64
TAIT 1
TANNER 26 31
TAYLOR 46 47
TENESEN, TENISON 30
TENNESSEE 47
TENNEY 9
TERNEY 56
TERRY 35
THOLINGS 40 41
THOMAS 62+
THOMPSON 13 14 33
THOMPSONS CREEK 50
THORN 18 19
THORNELL 19
THORNTON 20 21
THROCKMORTON 61
TIM (slave) 51
TINA (slave) 56
TODD 50+
TOM (slave) 56
TOM TERRY (slave) 16
TOMLINSON 1 3 16 30 49 51
TOTENTS 12
TREAVEANER 32
TREVINO 11 12 16 38
TRISLY 7
TRUDEAU 20 31
TRUE BLUE (slave) 31 32
TRULY 7 8 9 18 60 62 64 67
TUEL 49
TURNBULL 39
TURNER 11
TURPIN 21 53+
TYLER 42 48
VANCE 54
VAUCHERI 31
VIDAL 47 49 50 51 67
VILLA GAYOSO DISTRICT 30 47 49 50 57 58
VIRGINIA (state) 10 18 42 46 61 67
VOUCHERE 42
VOUSDAN 5 6 11 14 15 16 19 20 29 31 36 37 38 44 45 48 49 59 64
WADE 39 40 41

WALKER 42 43 44+ 45 50 54 59
WALL 64
WALTER 43
WALTMAN 52
WASHINGTON COUNTY 46
WATROUS 47
WATSON 48
WEEKS 8 53 65
WELCH 39 40
WELLS 13 14 15 44 58 66
WELSH 5
WELTON 23 29
WEST 12+ 35 36 39 40 47 48 50 61
WHEETLEY, WHETLEY 31
WHITAKER 39
WHITE 16 17+ 30 38 51 52
WHITE CLIFFS 18 19 32 55
WHITEHEAD 40
WHITES CREEK 43
WHITLEY 31
WICKES, WICKS 65 66
WIKOFF 60
WILKENS 42
WILKINS 45 46 51 54 63
WILL (slave) 27 28
WILLCOX 59 60
WILLIAM (slave) 30
WILLIAMS 9 16 30 44-46+ 55 62 65
WILLING 2 12 15 18 19 52
WILLIS 66
WILSON 9 40 41 47
WILTON 5 41 42
WIMBESH, WIMBUSH 24
WINFRE 6
WINFRED 20
WINFREE 14 15
WINSLOW 13 14 15
WOODS 32 33
WOOLEY, WOOLLEY 38 64
WOOTLEY 38
WYATT 15
WYLIE 59 60
YARBROUGH 51
YOULTNEY 10
YOUNG TOM (slave) 19
ZARIPA (slave) 32

Other Heritage Books by Carol Wells:

Abstracts of Giles County, Tennessee: County Court Minutes, 1813–1816 and Circuit Court Minutes, 1810–1816

CD: Tennessee, Volume 1

Davidson County, Tennessee County Court Minutes, Volume 1, 1783–1792

Davidson County, Tennessee County Court Minutes, Volume 2, 1792–1799

Davidson County, Tennessee County Court Minutes, Volume 3, 1799–1803

Dickson County, Tennessee County and Circuit Court Minutes, 1816–1828 and Witness Docket

Edgefield County, South Carolina Probate Records, Boxes One through Three Packages 1–106

Edgefield County, South Carolina Probate Records, Boxes Four through Six Packages 107–218

Edgefield County, South Carolina: Deed Books 13, 14 and 15

Edgefield County, South Carolina: Deed Books 16, 17 and 18

Edgefield County, South Carolina: Deed Books 19, 20, 21 and 22

Edgefield County, South Carolina: Deed Books 23, 24, 25 and 26

Edgefield County, South Carolina: Deed Books 27, 28 and 29

Edgefield County, South Carolina: Deed Books 30 and 31

Edgefield County, South Carolina: Deed Books 32 and 33

Edgefield County, South Carolina: Deed Books 34 and 35

Edgefield County, South Carolina: Deed Books 36, 37 and 38

Edgefield County, South Carolina: Deed Books 39 and 40

Edgefield County, South Carolina: Deed Book 41

Edgefield County, South Carolina: Deed Books 42 and 43, 1826–1829

Genealogical Abstracts of Edgefield, South Carolina Equity Court Records

Natchez Postscripts, 1781–1798

Rhea County, Tennessee Circuit Court Minutes, September 1815–March 1836

Rhea County, Tennessee Tax Lists, 1832–1834, and County Court Minutes Volume D: 1829–1834

Robertson County, Tennessee Court Minutes, 1796–1807

Rutherford County, Tennessee Court Minutes, 1811–1815

Sumner County, Tennessee Court Minutes, 1787–1805 and 1808–1810

Williamson County, Tennessee County Court Minutes, July 1812–October 1815

Williamson County, Tennessee County Court Minutes, May 1806–April 1812

www.ingramcontent.com/pod-product-compliance
Lightning Source LLC
Chambersburg PA
CBHW071109090426
42737CB00013B/2546
9781556136047